Martha the Hairpreneur

by Jane R. Plitt

and

Sally Valentine

Dedicated to

Martha Matilda Harper and her extraordinary

accomplishment.

May her spirit continue to inspire people to

use business

for social change.

May her achievements encourage all—

regardless of hardship—

to dare to make their dreams come true.

Introduction

Imagine a girl with ambition, but no hope because she was poor and, in fact, a servant for twenty-five years from the time she was seven! This is a story about just such a girl. However, that girl did not remain a servant. She seized opportunity, as this tale explains, and changed her life and the lives of thousands of others like you.

When we heard Martha's story, each of us became a life-long fan of this fabulous woman. We decided that young adults needed to know about her, and we hope that she will help guide you to fulfill your own potential.

While the story presented takes some liberties and is therefore historical fiction, it is based on the extraordinary life of Martha Matilda Harper, a Canadian immigrant who pioneered franchising and social entrepreneurship. She even invented the first reclining shampoo chair in the world!

Whatever your age, gender, or economic background, we hope that Martha will continue to inspire you—just as she has us. May you always feel her spirit supporting you and urging you to pursue your dreams.

Jane Plitt and Sally Valentine

Chapter 1

Servant Girl
1864

"No! No! Don't make me go."Martha sobbed and ran behind her mother, trying to hide in her skirt, but her father would have none of that. "Beady, let that girl go. I told you that this is what we have to do. You'd think she was being killed or something instead of being given an opportunity."

Beady pulled Martha into one last embrace. "You've got to do this for the family, Martha Matilda Harper." Beady slowly walked toward the waiting carriage, dragging her seven-year-old daughter with her.

Robert Harper didn't give Martha another chance to step away. He snatched her up and practically threw her into the waiting carriage. "No nonsense now, Daughter. You'd better work hard. Make us proud of you. We'll be looking for your earnings from Uncle John. Your mother and your brother and sisters are depending on you." He turned and walked away without looking back. Her mother stood still, slumped in defeat, one hand bravely waving until Martha could see her no more.

Martha's tears dried up as the carriage got moving. She found that she needed all of her strength to just hang on. More than once she felt like she was going to be thrown right off the seat and over the edge of the carriage—the carriage that was taking her away from her family and the small, one-room log cabin in Munn's Corners, Ontario, where she and her siblings all lived.

After one particularly hard jolt, Martha landed on the carriage floor. The driver glanced behind, but he didn't even slow down. I might as well stay here, she thought. The wooden floor was harder than the leather seat, but the rigid sides made it feel safer. Martha wound a lock of chestnut-colored hair around her finger and stroked her face with it. That was how she had comforted herself at home when she had heard her parents arguing, and that gave her comfort now. In spite of the constant jostling, she fell asleep.

Martha didn't know how to tell time, but it was just after sunrise when they left, and the sun seemed to be directly overhead when they stopped to change horses. "We'll take a break here," the driver said. "You can go inside to eat the food your mother gave you. Mrs. Spencer will be out to get you."

"C'mon down, child. I'll get you a cup of water and show you where you can relieve yourself."

Martha was glad to get out of the carriage. She walked in the direction Mrs. Spencer pointed, used the outhouse, and then came back to sit on the stoop to eat her hunk of bread and butter.

"That all you got, girl?"

Martha nodded. She didn't tell Mrs. Spencer that some days she didn't even get that to eat. "Here, eat this apple and take this piece of cheese with you. I understand you've still got thirty miles to go 'til you get to Leskard. You might get hungry again before you get there."

The driver whistled and waved, and Martha knew it was time to get back in the carriage. This time getting in, Martha really noticed the carriage. Why, the wheels are as tall as I am, she thought. She'd never ridden in a carriage before. The driver lifted her back inside, more gently than her father had. The carriage had two seats—driver in front, Martha in back. As they got underway, Martha tried to watch the scenery, but whenever she stuck her head out, the dust went up her nose and down her throat, making her cough. Finally, she wound a lock of hair around her finger and stroked her face with it, comforting herself again.

Martha woke to the sound of many voices. "Come out here, girl. I'm your uncle, John Gifford. Let's get a look at you."

While Uncle John and the others were looking at her, she was also busy looking at them. Uncle John was almost as wide as the carriage, with a big, deep voice. "Martha Matilda, this is my wife, Elsie Marie, and your two aunts, Roby Ann and Rannie."

Martha managed to say, "Hello, Ma'am," to each in turn, just as her mother had instructed her. The three women nodded but didn't speak—at least not to her. They turned their heads sideways and whispered secrets to each other. Martha couldn't take her eyes off of their dresses. Each wore a different color—blue, green, and dark pink. Martha self-consciously tried to brush off the dirt from her own plain dress, but even with the dirt brushed away, the dress was still brown.

Another woman, this one older, slowly approached the carriage. "Martha Matilda." It was her uncle's voice again. "This is your grandmother, Thursay Pickle. You do understand that you'll be in service to us all." It was more of a statement than a question. At seven years old, Martha did not understand everything that was happening, but she started to giggle. Grandmother Pickle looked just like a sour pickle.

"What's so funny, girl?" her grandmother asked. Her voice reminded Martha of the crows that shrieked in the cornfields behind her home in Munn's Corners.

She bit back another giggle, looked down at her shoes, and said, "Nothing, Ma'am."

Then Uncle John's scary voice interrupted her thoughts. "I'll show you to your room, Martha Matilda. You'll find some supper saved on the dresser for you. Get to bed quickly. We'll expect you to start working tomorrow. You'll need to rise before sunrise, start the fire in the kitchen, and gather eggs for breakfast."

"Is that when we all eat?" Martha asked.

Uncle John retorted, "Girl, you eat later, away from us. When we eat, you clean the chamber pots."

Martha wanted to ask how, since her mother had done that chore at home, but dared not. Instead, she went to her room, sat down on the small chair, and pulled the supper plate onto her lap. She wasn't sure what she was eating, but she was hungry, and it tasted good. What should she do with the dirty plate? Should she take it back to the kitchen? Where was the kitchen? This house had so many rooms, she might get lost. And for sure she didn't want to confront Uncle John again.

She laid the plate on the dresser and took off her traveling clothes—not sure what to do with them either. She dropped them on the floor and slipped on her nightdress, one of the few things in her bag. Then she took out her brush and sat on her bed—her bed. She'd never had a bed all to herself before. She thought of her brother and sisters at home, wishing she were there, too. As tears welled up in her eyes, she unfastened her braid and shook her hair loose. Then she grabbed the brush tightly and started pulling it through her thick mane. She counted one, two, three … Lonely and afraid, Martha was long past one hundred before she was calm enough to fall asleep.

Chapter 2

Life in Leskard

"Get up, you lazy brat," Uncle John screamed. "I told you to get the fire going before sunrise."

Martha wiped away her dried tears and said, "Right away, Uncle John."

Freezing, Martha pulled on her day dress, wool socks, and sweater and scampered into the kitchen where Uncle John met her with a huge whack on her fanny. "This is never to happen again, girl. Get going."

Looking around, Martha saw the wood and began to throw it on the fireplace.

Uncle John screamed, "Didn't your mother teach you anything? You start a fire by gathering up the embers. You need dry twigs and leaves at the bottom, then larger pieces, kindling, and fuel," he lectured as he demonstrated the art of fire building.

Martha watched wide-eyed. It had been her older brother Ephraim's job to build fires, not hers. She saw her uncle light the fire and blow on the bottom to fan the flames. It seemed magical to her, but she gulped as she realized from here on, she would be the fire maker.

Next, she got the eggs from the chicken coop, shooing away the chickens, the way her mother had done. She started to cry. "Mama, I miss you," she blurted out, but then quickly choked back her tears when she headed toward the house. "I am alone, aren't I, Mama?" she said to her mother who wasn't there. Why do I have to call this man "uncle," she wondered. Uncle John doesn't act like family. He is my master. I am his servant. Her tears started to flow again.

Hearing Martha whimper as she entered, Uncle John got up from the table and whacked her again. "If you need something to cry about, I will give it to you." Martha bawled—dropping the eggs.

Uncle John turned red and removed his belt and beat her until Elsie Marie, his wife, said, "Enough, John. She is young." With a harrumph, he put his belt back and left the room. Instantly, Martha crawled to the corner.

"Clean that mess up, Martha," Elsie Marie ordered, taking charge now. "There's a pail and mop around the corner."

Martha dutifully followed her instructions, going to the well for water and mopping the eggs up. She squeezed her hands on the water bucket and the mop handle as tightly as she could to ease the pain of the welts popping up on her back.

"There will be nothing for your breakfast, Martha, but some dry toast. There are consequences for your carelessness," Elsie Marie continued. It was clear to Martha her aunt was second in charge, and not a kindly person, in spite of her intervention.

"Now get the chamber pots and empty them in the outhouse. Don't spill them, or I will make you drink the rest!"

Martha followed Aunt Elsie's instructions, but outside it was so cold that she wanted to hurry. She spilled some on her shoes. "Oh, God, no!" she screamed. She rubbed her shoes in the grass trying to clean them before she re-entered the house. "No more tears, Martha," she whispered to herself. Then, as if making a sacred pledge, she added, "Someday, you will be happy."

Not every day was as bad as that first day. Being quick and observant, Martha began to learn how to please this family. But she was not pleased with her life. Martha never went to school, nor did she have formal lessons at home. It would be 1871 before school attendance was compulsory in Ontario, Canada. Her life was simply work, work, and more work.

When her breakfast chores were over, Martha had to fetch water from the well for the aunts' washbasins. Then she had to help them dress. Grandmother Pickle needed the most help. Grandmother's weak arms couldn't reach up very high, and her stiff back kept her from bending over very low. Martha had to sit on the floor to pull up Grandmother's stockings and squeeze her feet into her shoes. This process was difficult for both Martha and her grandmother.

They were both happy when Grandmother was dressed, and they could move on to her hair. First, Martha would comb out the nighttime tangles and then brush what was left of Grandmother's thinning head of hair.

"What I wouldn't give for hair like yours, Martha," Grandma would say to her. That was about as close to a compliment as Martha could expect—either from her aunts or her grandmother.

Her aunts were called spinsters by the townspeople. The way they said it made being a spinster sound like a bad thing. Martha eventually found out that a spinster was just someone who didn't have a husband. Martha came to know the aunts as her bosses, and mean bosses at that. They offered no love, just orders.

"Yes, Ma'am," was her expected response to their demands. Martha said the right words, but her stomach was doing flip-flops. She missed her mother; it was her father who had sent her away. She knew that her mother was as helpless as she. As time went on, Martha swore she would never marry and let a man control her life—even if it meant being called a spinster like her aunts.

Although her aunts and grandmother had a much better life than her mother, Martha knew that it was Uncle

John who had the last say. As she observed life in Leskard and overheard many conversations, it became clear to her that men controlled everything.

"John, what do you think about this year's wheat crop?" townsmen would ask him. No one asked her aunts and grandmother their opinions. It was the men who made the money, and if women worked, they had to turn it over to their father, husband, or uncle. They couldn't own property, not like her Uncle John, who owned both a clover mill and a grain elevator.

Men had power, and Martha was powerless now. But, each night as she crawled into her bed, she would fantasize about her future. She silently told herself, "Someday I, too, will be important; my opinions will be listened to; and I won't hurt anyone. In fact, I am going to be especially kind and help other poor girls and their mommies."

Meanwhile, she watched Uncle John strut around town with his chest puffed out, patting other merchants on the back as if they were friends; but Martha knew he did not like them. He was a showman. Oh, and when they celebrated the defeat of the Irish Catholics at the Battle of the Boyne, he would get dressed in costume and lead the parade as the "head toot" of the Protestant men of the local Orange Society. As her Uncle John marched, Martha thought the Irish Catholics were like her—defeated. Would any of them be able to rise up and shout back, "This is not fair"?

The work never ended in the Gifford household. Some of the work was the same every day, but other work changed with the seasons. In the winter, the floor had to be mopped every time someone came in, and Martha had to polish everyone's boots. In the summer, the rugs had to be taken outside to hang on the line and be beaten. Canning season started in August with corn, peaches, tomatoes, and beans put away for winter. Martha learned to smile, to make believe she was an obedient servant. She tried her best, which often was not good enough. The worst part was that her meager pay of $3 or $4 a month went directly to her father, the lazy tailor who liked to pretend to be a gentleman.

Visits to see her family were few and far between. She learned that her siblings had been bound out into servitude just as she was. The stomach pains inside her grew. She was furious with her father, but powerless to do anything about it. Once when she went back for Christmas after being away two years, her mother greeted her with tears. "There's no money for a holiday celebration, Mattie. Guess we will just have to be it." Her father, Robert, appeared late—too busy to see his children.

"I hate him!" she silently yelled, but dared not say what was in her mind. Trust no one but yourself, Martha Matilda, she told herself.

At night, alone and scared in her room, Martha would grab onto her long locks, holding them as if they were her only support. She brushed and brushed her hair as if brushing out the weariness, the insults, and the loneliness of the day. With no mother or mother-figure to comfort her, she learned how to comfort herself. The rhythmic brushing relaxed her until she was ready to sleep—the sleep restoring her to face another day of work.

"When I grow up, I am going to be free," she assured herself and her pillow.

Chapter 3

The German Doctor

"What do they think I am," fumed Martha, "a piece of furniture?" Martha was packing up her things—not that she owned much of anything besides the cotton housedress, stockings, and sturdy shoes she was wearing. At the age of twelve, without any say in the matter, Martha was being uprooted again. Not given any details, all Martha knew was that from then on she would be in service to a European physician and his sickly wife in the nearby town of Orono, Ontario. Although not exactly a slave, she was being treated more like a commodity than a person.

Luckily for Martha, the man who met her carriage this time was like neither her father nor her uncle. Martha was pleasantly surprised when she found out that Dr. Herriman, her new employer, was a kindly gentleman, who was also an herbalist. He actually kissed her hand and slightly bowed to her as he said, "Enchanted!" Martha wanted to giggle, but she had mastered pushing her real emotions down into her stomach. She simply nodded.

The Herrimans' house was different than Uncle John's. It was separated into two parts. Dr. Herriman and his wife lived in the back of the house. The front of the house was given over to Dr. Herriman's medical practice, and he gave her a tour while spelling out her duties.

"This is my reception area, Martha." He pointed at a wood-burning stove. "You'll be expected to light the fire first thing in the morning so my patients will be comfortable. You'll also be expected to keep the room as clean as our personal sitting room. In the winter this may require mopping the floor several times a day. Verstehen Sie?"

"Yes, doctor." She had done all of this at Uncle John's.

"Here is the examining room. You will clean this at the end of every day. I will give you a special cleaning solution to use on all of the surfaces. Cleanliness is the doctor's friend."

Martha nodded.

"That brings us to my office. He opened a door into a sunlit room with tied-back drapes, a glass chandelier, an Oriental rug, and a desk as big as the table in her home in Munn's Corners. Martha's mouth fell open, but it wasn't because of the desk. She couldn't take her eyes off of the walls. They were covered in books. Her eyes leapt from wall to wall and shelf to shelf. There must be over five hundred books here, she thought. Oh, if only I could read.

Dr. Herriman must have been reading her mind. "You seem to be taken by my library, Martha. Do you read?"

Martha looked down at her shoes. "No, but I'd like to learn." Oh, I shouldn't have said that, she thought. Was I being too bold?

"Maybe we can do something about that," Dr. Herriman said. My last housekeeper hated these books. Too much to dust, she complained."

"I don't mind dusting them," Martha answered quickly.

"I'll expect this room cleaned once a week. He looked sternly at Martha. Just don't disturb anything on my desk. Verstehen Sie?"

"Yes, doctor."

With a sweep of his hand and a slight bow, Dr. Herriman ushered Martha out of his office. "Now, there's one more room, but it will be off-limits to you. That is my Laboratorium, where I make up all my healing ointments and salves and elixirs.

Even with the door closed, Martha could detect a slight odor. She had a hundred questions, but she was afraid to ask them. Uncle John always said that she asked too many questions. She swallowed her curiosity and simply said, "Do I understand you correctly that I am not to clean in there at all, doctor?"

"Ja, never. In fact I keep it locked."

Martha settled into a new routine. Mrs. Herriman was sometimes demanding, but not mean in the way her aunts were. Martha knew that she should be glad she didn't have to clean das Labor, but the closed door intrigued her. Dr. Herriman's behavior intrigued her, too. When behind the closed door he often whistled or sang, in German of course. Dr. Herriman is happy in das Labor, she thought.

After she had been there a year, Martha's curiosity got the best of her. Mrs. Herriman was having a good day, and Dr. Herriman thought it would do her good to get outside in the country. He arranged for a carriage ride.

While they were gone, Martha paced in front of the closed door. She thought she had seen Dr. Herriman leave without locking up because he was so concerned with the outing. Finally, Martha reached for the doorknob. I'll just see if it's locked, she thought. She turned the knob left then right. It moved freely. Don't go in, she said to herself. Who will know, she answered back. Bong, bong, bong! The long case clock in the waiting area chimed three. In the quiet house, the noise startled her so that she jumped, and the door seemed to open on its own.

Martha tiptoed into the room. Why was she tiptoeing? She knew that no one was around to hear her. Inside, there was only a sliver of light from a small, high window. As her eyes adjusted to the dark, Martha slowly surveyed the room. This was like being at the outdoor market. She recognized mint leaves in a box on one shelf and rosemary on another. She saw thistle and feverfew.

Braver now, she picked up a root and put it to her nose. Ah, ginger. There were also bottles of all sizes, some full, some empty. Some of the contents looked thin and clear like alcohol. Others look thick and cloudy like olive oil. A work bench ran the length of the room. There was a stool underneath it.

Martha pulled out the stool and climbed up on it. This is meant for someone much taller than I am, she thought. On the bench there was a marble bowl. Martha gently picked it up and rubbed her hands over it. It felt cold and smooth. Next to it was a thick, stirring stick. A mortar and pestle, Martha thought. She had heard about those. That's how Dr. Herriman mixes his tonics.

In fact, on the shelf directly above was a bottle with some leaves suspended in a liquid. What could that be? She reached out to examine it more closely. The outside of the bottle felt oily. Oops! The bottle fell out of her hand and onto the wood floor. She climbed off of the stool into a pool of oil. There were pieces of broken glass everywhere. Now what? She ran to the kitchen in the back of the house to get cleaning rags.

Chapter 4

A Secret Formula

Martha knew she'd have to tell Dr. Herriman what had happened. He'd certainly miss the bottle of tonic or notice the glass in the trash. What if he fired her? Would she have to go back to her uncle's house or to live with some stranger who was even worse?

As soon as Mrs. Herriman was settled back in bed, Martha confessed. She showed her master the stain on the floor and the remains of the bottle in the trash. Dr. Herriman was not happy. "Martha, haven't I told you over and over not to disturb the work in das Labor?"

"Yes, doctor."

"And haven't I treated you well?"

"Yes, doctor."

"Go to your quarters now, Martha. I will think on what to do about this."

"Yes, doctor." Martha's chin quivered, but she would not cry. She had gotten very good at suppressing her emotions.

For the next few days, Martha went about her chores as quietly as possible, avoiding Dr. Herriman whenever she could. On payday, he confronted her. "Come into my office, Martha. Sit down." He motioned to her to sit on the other side of the desk from him. Martha had never sat there before. She put her hand on her leg to keep it from twitching.

"Martha, I cannot overlook an act of disobedience, but I'm afraid that letting you go would hurt me as much as it hurts you. Except for this one time, you have been a good employee, diligent about your work. I've decided to keep you on, but you will find your pay envelope short by the amount it will cost me to replace what you broke. Verstehen Sie?"

"Yes, doctor. Thank you, doctor."

"And you must promise not to enter das Labor again."

"I promise, doctor."

Some time passed before Dr. Herriman called Martha into his office again. What did I do now? she wondered. I've been trying so hard to please him.

"Martha, I've been noticing your hair."

"My hair?" She unconsciously reached out and wrapped a strand around her finger.

"Yes, I can see that you spend time brushing it, and brushing is good. The more you brush your hair, the stronger it becomes because of the increase of blood flow. You must stimulate the scalp. But also, Martha, you must wash your hair more often. I'm going to give you some of my special herbal tonic. I'm starting to think that your interest in my Laboratorium is not such a bad thing. Make sure you rub the scalp vigorously."

Martha wasn't sure what to think. This was not how she had taken care of her aunts' hair. It was totally opposite to the Victorian manner of rarely washing hair, maybe once or twice a year, and using powder to clean it in between washings. But she was very happy that Dr. Herriman seemed to have forgiven her sneaking into das Labor.

From then on, Dr. Herriman shared with Martha more and more of his scientific knowledge. He explained to her that his beliefs of blending western medicine with homeopathic methods were different than most Canadian doctors. "Martha, I am an outsider and will always be one. My accent makes me different, but so do my beliefs. First, we must listen to the body and encourage it to work. It is a magnificent machine, but sometimes we forget how to encourage the life force to flow. Keep stimulating your scalp. Brush hard. You need to feel your head prickle."

Martha listened to Dr. Herriman because he was a man who treated Martha like a person, not a dishrag. This was a man who spoke like a teacher, not like an overseer.

Martha didn't think twice about following his directions for growing beautiful hair. The results were amazing. Her hair got more beautiful and grew stronger and longer. In fact, it grew so long that it eventually touched the floor. Once a source of comfort, Martha's hair was now becoming a source of pride. Although she was less than five-feet tall, her hair gave her stature and status. By letting it down, in long pigtails, she sent a message to the world that she was unconventional, looking for adventure, and wanting to be noticed.

Her whole personality was summed up in that head of thick, shiny, healthy, flowing, long hair. This was in stark contrast to her mother, and many other women of her day, who wore their hair tightly pulled back in a bun. The bun reflected those lives which were reined in, confined to one place, and unnoticed.

When Dr. Herriman's wife died, Martha moved with him to Port Hope in Ontario. Ultimately, she worked for him for over ten years. Dr. Herriman was cultured and poised. Martha admired his refinement and class. Unconsciously, she took on some of his continental mannerisms. Besides sharing his scientific beliefs, Dr. Herriman even gave Martha the opportunity to learn how to read and write during her time there.

Although Dr. Herriman was an understanding boss, Martha was still in service and had to work hard. She kept holding onto her locks of hair and dreaming of a time when she would be working for herself and not someone else. She had learned from experience that women without their own money were subject to others telling them what to do. A friend told her that one day her hair would make her fortune. Martha held onto that dream.

She also dreamed of a new life in a new place. Martha saw a postcard from a friend of Dr. Herriman's. It came from Rochester, NY, a city across Lake Ontario. Martha fantasized about this place she had never been. The postcard painted a picture of a land of promise, of action, of opportunity. Dr. Herriman let her keep it, and Martha taped the picture to the wall of her room. She looked at it every morning and evening. It became her Mecca.

As Martha was dreaming about her new life, Dr. Herriman became sick. He called Martha to his bedside.

"Martha, you know I'm very ill." Dr. Herriman was half-lying and half-sitting in his bed. He leaned over and coughed into a spittoon.

"It's okay, Dr. Herriman. You don't have to talk."

"But I have something to give you." He coughed again. "Take the key to das Labor."

Martha let out a gasp. "Are you telling me to go into your Laboratorium?"

"Yes. Now, get the key from my dresser. Go to das Labor. On the top shelf..." His voice was so low, she could hardly hear him.

"...there's a box. Bring it here."

"Yes, doctor." Martha hurried off and back.

"Open it."

"It's for you," Dr. Herriman said when Martha pulled a piece of paper out of the box, "to make good in America. You've always ..." He coughed again. "... hard worker ... make a future."

Martha unfolded the paper, and there in Dr. Herriman's handwriting was the secret formula for his special hair tonic. Martha couldn't believe her good fortune. This gift was better than money. "Thank you! Thank ..." She looked over at Dr. Herriman. He was already asleep.

It wasn't long before Dr. Herriman died.

This is my chance, Martha thought. She gathered her courage and inquired about servant jobs in Rochester, across the Great Lake. After all, being a household servant was the only thing she had been trained to do. She was soon hired by the Hovey family, but this time Martha was not being handed off like a piece of furniture. This time Martha was choosing where and for whom she would work. This time Martha was taking charge of her future.

Martha made her way to the New Hope pier. It couldn't have had a better name. In 1882, at the age of twenty-five, Martha Matilda Harper said goodbye to Canada and boarded the steamship *Norseman* for a new life in America. She took with her a job offer, a brown jug filled with hair tonic, the secret formula for the tonic, and a knotted handkerchief that held sixty hard-earned silver dollars (her life savings). She walked up the gangplank alone.

The rough waters of Lake Ontario crashed against the boat's hull as she boarded. Just for a moment she thought back to that first carriage ride, how her father had thrown her into the carriage. She threw back her shoulders and lifted her chin. This trip was different. She strode forward.

Once onboard, Martha was confronted with a cacophony of new sights and sounds. She didn't expect it to be this loud. People milled all around, shouting to be heard above the noise of the ship's engine. Chickens cackled and goats brayed, but she didn't care. Martha beamed. She was on her way to a new life.

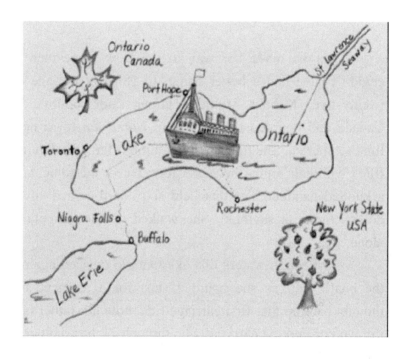

Chapter 5

A New Start in a New Country

When the ship docked in Rochester, Martha could not immediately get off. Impatiently she waited in a long line of people who had to state their business, answer questions, and sign forms before being allowed to disembark. Finally, the Harbor Master said, "Welcome to the United States," and Martha was able to leave the boat in a wave of people who all seemed to be in as great a hurry as she.

Her head was spinning like an exhausted top at half speed as she lugged her jug and the carpetbag holding her worldly possessions down the boardwalk. Martha kept repeating to herself, "I am in the United States of America. I am in the United States of America." Then she heard a woman shouting. Looking up, she saw someone holding a sign that said, "Martha Matilda Harper."

Someone is here for me, she thought. Mrs. Hovey, her mistress, introduced herself and never stopped talking. "Our carriage is waiting for you. We have a bit of a ride to get to our home." Martha was almost speechless, but managed to smile and nod in an appreciative manner.

Martha observed Mrs. Hovey. She was dressed smartly, not flamboyantly, which was the way of the rich. Mrs. Hovey was treating this ride as an educational tour and continued bragging about her hometown.

"Rochester is a hotbed of manufacturing. We make things happen here. Look over there. That's the eyeglass factory started by John Jacob Bausch and Henry Lomb. They're German immigrants, you know."

Am I an immigrant, too? Martha wondered.

"See how it backs up to the river. That's the Genesee River, and right on the other side, Joseph Requa demonstrated to the government the machine gun he invented."

Machine gun? What's that? Martha's mind was reeling.

Mrs. Hovey didn't seem to notice. She ran on. "Speaking of inventing, Mr. Hovey's friend George, George Eastman, that is, is experimenting with photography. He talks of opening a factory, too."

"What church do you attend, Martha?"

Martha opened her mouth to answer, but Mrs. Hovey just kept on talking.

"It doesn't matter. You'll find that all our churches here support each other." She lowered her voice. "We even have Jews who live here. Then there are the Quakers. They're a small, but strong group. Am I correct in assuming you've heard of them?"

Martha didn't even try to answer this time, and Mrs. Hovey continued. "The Quakers keep advocating for social justice. They brought Frederick Douglas here where he published his paper, the *North Star*. Believe you me— that caused quite a stir, supporting abolition and all." Mrs. Hovey started to cough.

"What about the women in Rochester?"

"What's that you said? This road dust makes me cough."

Did I say that out loud? Martha wondered. "I was just thinking about the women, Mrs. Hovey. What are the women of Rochester like?"

"There are women like me, Martha, with, let's say a certain social standing and, of course, servant girls such as yourself. But then there are also the 'Suffragists.' Why, do you know that right near here, in 1848, in a town called Seneca Falls, one hundred people gathered for a women's rights convention and signed a Declaration of Sentiments. They were calling for a woman's right to vote.

"That same year, Rochester women organized a Working Woman's Protective Union, declaring that women had just as much right to be in the workplace as men. To top it off, in 1872, Susan B. Anthony and other women challenged the voting laws, and Anthony was arrested for registering and voting in the presidential election right here in Rochester. Susan B. Anthony still lives here and is engaged in women's rights. Oh, yes, there are lots of people stirring up folks with their newfangled ideas here. Harrumph!" Martha noted Mrs. Hovey's deep breath.

After that, Mrs. Hovey started talking about the house and the chores. Martha tried very hard to pay attention to her words, but she was still thinking of the "Suffragists." Women declaring they have rights? Women wanting to vote and to work like men? Martha wanted to know more, but Mrs. Hovey was going on about the silver tea set.

By the time Martha reached the Hovey home at 881 East Main Street, she had certainly heard about Rochester as a home to inventors and bold women. And it was so big. What was it Mrs. Hovey just said? The city had ninety thousand people? It sounded promising, like the Mecca she had pictured back in Canada, but she knew at the moment she had to become a treasured servant.

Martha started looking around the Hoveys' house from a servant's perspective. She was very impressed by the outside of the two-story Victorian home with the glass cupola. The inside was equally elegant, but Martha was not anticipating sitting on one of those Victorian sofas that looked awfully stiff. Martha was still a servant. She was looking at the silver that would need polishing and the carpets that would need beating. What was it that Mrs. Hovey said about her tea service? At least they have indoor plumbing, she thought.

When she was shown to her bedroom, she secreted her jug of hair tonic carefully under the bed. Then she looked around again before taking out her brush and starting the familiar routine that had comforted her so often. "One, two, three…" she started counting the strokes aloud, remembering dear Dr. Herriman and his advice. "Blood flow, Martha, keep brushing." She heard it over and over in her ear.

Chapter 6

Another Change

"Mrs. Hovey, what else can I do for you today?" Martha asked one morning after serving her mistress breakfast.

"Oh, Martha, my hair! I need to meet Luther for lunch today, and I must look like the wife of an important Rochester lawyer."

"Where will you be dining?" Martha asked.

"Oh, at the Powers Grill! Then I will go to the Powers' Art Gallery, where I will meet up with my friend, Mrs. Sibley.

"Mrs. Hovey, who is she?"

"Oh, Martha, you need to learn so much. Her husband started Western Union with Ezra Cornell. Luther does work for Hiram."

"Are they friends with Mr. Cutler, the one who was talking about constructing a mail chute?" Martha learned a lot by listening intently (some people would call it eavesdropping) to conversations when the Hoveys had parties.

"Yes, we're all friends." Oh, everyone is connected here in Rochester, Martha thought. What was it Mrs. Hovey called it? Making a network?

"Martha, dress my hair so all will admire me. Your special hair tonic really does make my hair shine."

"Of course, Ma'am," Martha said, smiling to herself. Someday people will know my product and talent, and it goes far beyond pleasing a mistress. Meanwhile, Martha bided her time and learned more and more about her new community. And so, among these inventive, free-thinking people who were not afraid of social change, Martha found a home. That's why she was so upset a year after her arrival when Mrs. Hovey told her they were moving.

"Not again!" Martha couldn't help the words escaping from her mouth.

"What's that, dear?" Mrs. Hovey said.

"Nothing, Ma'am. I just wondered where we're moving to."

"*We* are not moving anywhere, Martha. Just Luther and I will be moving. You'll be staying on with the house."

Martha didn't know how to feel about that. On the one hand, she didn't want to be uprooted again, just when she was getting used to this home. On the other hand, she didn't like feeling like part of the furniture again—just some wooden thing that came with the house.

"Yes, Ma'am," Martha replied. Inside she felt her stomach turning again, and again she resolved to one day become independent.

The names of the couple who moved into Mr. and Mrs. Hovey's house were Owen and Luella Roberts. They were a handsome couple, who dressed well to fit their place in society. The Roberts had no children, and both had been orphaned early in life. They were rich in material goods but lacking in emotional stability. Martha had to tend to their physical needs as well as their need for love and affection. In doing so, Martha became the dutiful daughter they never had, and Mrs. Roberts became the mother figure that Martha had to leave behind. In other words, they became family to each other. Martha finally had a real home, and she would live with the Roberts until they died.

But the Roberts had their problems, too. It soon became evident that Mr. Roberts was an alcoholic, and Martha felt compelled to protect Mrs. Roberts in a way she could not protect her own mother, Beady. Martha made sure no significant harm came to Mrs. Roberts as a result of her husband's abuse.

Very often, their evenings ended like this: "Mr. Roberts, why don't you sit down and rest in the study," Martha would greet the master when he tumbled into the house late at night, after gambling and drinking. "Let me take your shoes and socks off, Sir," Martha coaxed him. "You must be too tired to go upstairs and sleep; I have made up a bed for you in your study," Martha explained, as she guided the wobbly Mr. Roberts in.

Mr. Roberts belched and then up-chucked his evening's food and drink. "No worry, Mr. Roberts, I will clean it up. Come along," Martha soothed him.

Standing on the stairs watching and whimpering was Mrs. Roberts. When Martha came back down, she put an arm around her boss. "Come, dear. Let's have ourselves a cup of tea."

"Martha, what would I do without you? You care about me the way no one else has ever cared for me. You're not simply a housemaid, Martha. You're family."

Martha's heart skipped when she heard Mrs. Roberts call her family. She, too, had felt it, but now it was confirmed. And now, there were more people for Martha to take care of. First, though, she needed a different life.

Chapter 7

A Business Plan

Mr. Roberts had investments in real estate and business, so Martha continued to come in contact with Rochester's elite. By being seen and helpful, but not heard, Martha learned who was important in local society.

Mrs. Roberts raved about Martha's hair treatments to these influential friends, and soon they asked Martha to dress their hair as well. They wanted the special tonic from Martha's secret formula. And it didn't stop there. Soon they also wanted scalp massages and facials. That gave Martha the idea that there might be a business in dressing people's hair and giving skin treatments at a shop instead of in the privacy of a lady's boudoir. She began to save her dollars in earnest and make the tonic in her bedroom. One day she was doing just that when Mrs. Roberts knocked on her closed door. "Martha, are you in there? I need your help with Mr. Roberts. He's fallen again."

"I'll be right there," Martha called. She put down the pestle in her hand and went to the door. She opened it a crack and tried to slide out, but Mrs. Roberts flung the door open in her effort to grab Martha and bring her along.

"What are you doing, and what's that smell?"

"Let's attend to Mr. Roberts, and I'll explain later," said Martha. The women hurried down the hall to help the master. Later Martha confessed that the mortar and pestle, the herbs and oils, had to do with the special tonic she used on Mrs. Roberts' hair.

"Well, Martha. I can't complain about your hair tonic. All the ladies rave about how beautiful my hair looks. But let me talk to Mr. Roberts. I think maybe the tonic would be best made out in the shed."

Martha knew that the tonic was her key to independence and success. Like many other female entrepreneurs, Martha didn't know exactly what form that success would take; she just knew that she had to pursue it. She got busy stirring up tonic in the Roberts's shed.

Martha bottled her tonic in brown jugs, called it "Mascaro Tonique" to sound exotic, and test marketed it by selling it door-to-door. Martha still had all of her duties at the Roberts's house too, so Mrs. Allen, a neighbor, agreed to help.

"I'll sell it for you, Martha," Mrs. Allen enthused. "I can give my personal testimony about what your Mascaro Tonique has done for my hair."

A few weeks later, Mrs. Allen was even more excited. "I've sold $2.50 worth this week. Let's celebrate."

Of course, Martha was glad to hear this news, but it wasn't enough. As her knowledge, reputation, and confidence grew, she started to envision a world turned upside down. It would be a world where she would no longer be at the beck and call of wealthy women; a world where wealthy women would come to her. She would open a salon where both men and women would come for scalp massages and hair treatments using products she had created. She would be her own boss, an American businesswoman.

Opening a beauty salon was a revolutionary idea at the time. There were no such salons in Rochester. Wealthy women were used to having their hair treated in the privacy of their own homes. That didn't deter Martha. She hired a lawyer.

"What brings you to my office, Miss Harper?" said John VanVoorhis.

"I'm going to establish a business."

"May I ask why you chose my office?"

"I heard that you represent George Selden, Frederick Douglass, and Susan B. Anthony, so I decided you must be the best lawyer in Rochester."

VanVoorhis chuckled. "If only everyone thought so, Miss Harper. What type of business are you proposing? Have you invented an engine like George Selden's?"

"No, of course not." Martha noted that he dropped the smile at her serious tone. "It will be a salon, a soothing, calming place where Rochester women will be able to come and be pampered. I will give scalp treatments and head and neck massages based on scientific principles. Then I will dress my customer's hair, letting the woman's natural beauty shine through. While I am working, I will also be doing my best to improve the customer's spirit. Mind, body and spirit are all connected, you know."

Mr. VanVoorhis thought for a moment. Then he spoke. "This is a revolutionary idea, Miss Harper. You will come up against some fierce resistance. Free thinkers always face opposition. Are you prepared for that?"

"Yes, I am, Mr. VanVoorhis."

"You have given this a lot of thought, haven't you?"

"Mr. VanVoorhis, I've been dreaming about this my whole life."

"Have you thought about a trademark?"

"Why, yes, I have. I want to use a cornucopia. You see, Mr. VanVoorhis, my logo will represent the horn of plenty. Anyone associated with my business will find her life full and overflowing with opportunity and success. Customers will be joyful, as will my associates."

"Just how will you fund this venture? George Eastman is about to launch KODAK with one million dollars in venture money. What do you have?"

Martha sat up straight, looked him in the eye, and said, "I have my lifetime savings of $360 and a determination to make this work."

Mr. VanVoorhis nodded, and said, "In that case, I am delighted to be your legal partner. May I shake your hand?"

Martha was ready for business, but just then she received another blow.

Chapter 8

Healing

Martha had been working too hard. She was still serving as a maid to the Roberts, while also preparing to open a shop and mixing up batches of her secret tonic. Martha was exhausted, and one day she simply collapsed.

"Martha! What's wrong, Martha?" Mrs. Roberts went running into the kitchen where Martha had been mopping the floor. "I thought I heard a moan. Oh, no, you've fallen. Can you sit up, dear?" she asked, putting an arm under Martha's back and helping her lean forward. "Now, don't try to stand, Martha. I'll just call the doctor."

"No! I don't want to see a doctor."

"But, Martha, you haven't been looking well lately. I was afraid something like this would happen."

Martha grabbed her head. "Maybe you're right. I've been trying to please you both and still prepare my

Mascaro Tonique for the opening of my store. I haven't gotten much sleep. I haven't been feeling well, and I might need help. But not your doctor, please. Call Mrs. Smith."

"Mrs. Smith? Is she a doctor? I know that Blackwell woman became a doctor, but I don't know of any female doctors in Rochester."

"No! I don't want a doctor. Helen Pine Smith is a Christian Science healing practitioner. I think she can make me well without a doctor. I just need prayer and a positive mental outlook. No drugs.

Martha had heard about Christian Science in 1888. It was a new religion, founded in 1879 by Mary Baker Eddy, who started her own quest to overcome illness. Instead of being treated with alcohol or drug-based remedies of the day that seemed to make her only sicker, Eddy began to pray and found renewed strength and wellness through prayer.

Eddy created a Mother Church in Boston, with satellite churches operating around the world. The satellite churches had to adhere to clear guidelines about when and what prayers would be read by which leader, called the "Reader." There were no ministers. The Mother Church published written instructions. Training for the satellite churches took place in Boston. There was no formal ministry, but rather all members could actively participate. Christian Scientists believed in the equality of men and women. This religion with its inclusive, loose structure and its focus on health and beauty was something Martha could embrace. It was just like Dr. Herriman's teachings. Health became beauty. Beauty came from health.

Mrs. Smith, a robust woman with a warm smile, came to treat Martha. They talked. Mrs. Smith took Martha's hands and held them as she closed her eyes. "Martha, look inward. Release the pain of the past. Know that the Spirit resides within. Feel the warmth of that Spirit and know you will never be alone again." They prayed together intensely.

Within three days, Martha felt well again. Martha became a member of the Christian Science church and remained so her whole life. She braided Christian Science beliefs in with her own beliefs. She believed that the outer body should reflect the inner body. She believed that beauty started with a positive mental attitude. Spirit, enhanced by natural tonics and healthy scalp massages, led to health and beauty. That combination worked for her. Why wouldn't it work for others, too?

The visits with Mrs. Smith, the healer, cost Martha precious money that she had saved up to start her business, but it also helped her form the principles that would guide her in business and eventually bring her tremendous success. Before too long, Martha was once again ready to open her first salon.

"See, Mrs. Roberts, I am better because I found my inner light, and it will shine on me as I become a businesswoman."

"Martha, I only wish I could believe that. You will succeed because you work hard and have something special to offer."

Not wanting to differ with her boss, Martha replied, "Mrs. Roberts, could it be both? Thank you for letting me live here while I prepare for my business launch."

"You are like my daughter. You will live with us forever. You are doing what I could never do. May you only succeed!"

"Thank you, Mrs. Roberts." To herself she added, if only.

Chapter 9

The First Salon

"It's good to see you again, Miss Harper." Mr. VanVoorhis stood up. Martha, wearing a borrowed pair of Mrs. Roberts's gloves, shook his hand. "Please sit down. How may I help you today? I can assure you that my son, Eugene, has applied for your trademark, and you'll be hearing from us soon about that. These things take time, you know."

"I'm not here about the trademark, Mr. VanVoorhis. I'm here to ask for your help in another matter. I'd like you to talk to Mr. Powers about renting me space in this building for my salon."

"I see. Have you spoken to Mr. Powers about renting space yet?"

"Yes, I have."

"And I take it you didn't receive a favorable response."

"That's correct. In fact, he was downright rude."

"What exactly did he say?"

"He said that there was no such beauty salon as I was proposing in Rochester."

"That's true."

"Yes, it is true. I want to be the first. He also said that powder, rouge, and other cosmetics were low class, inappropriate for proper women."

"I see."

"He thinks my salon will attract 'trollops and prostitutes,' his words exactly, and he doesn't want those kind of women in his building, bothering his tenants."

"There are other buildings in Rochester. Have you looked at other spaces? Perhaps another location would work ..."

"Mr. VanVoorhis," Martha interrupted. "I want my salon in THIS building. It's the tallest building in Rochester. It has gas illumination and marble floors, and it was built with fireproof materials. It even has an art gallery and an elevator. It is THE place to do business in Rochester because it attracts the finest people in town— people like you."

Mr. VanVoorhis was quiet for a moment. Martha thought she saw a bit of a blush under his white beard.

"You know, Sir, my salon will make Rochester a leader in the area of public beauty care."

"All right, Miss Harper. I'll speak to Mr. Powers on your behalf."

"Thank you, Mr. VanVoorhis. I can assure you and Mr. Powers both that I'll serve only the most proper people in my salon."

Had John VanVoorhis been swayed by Martha's business sense or by her beautiful, long hair? He didn't say. Either way, Martha got her space, Room 516 on the fifth floor of the Powers Building. But it was not without compromise. Daniel Powers would not give Martha a year-long lease. He insisted that Martha rent month-to-month so that he could evict her if the business attracted the wrong kind of women.

Martha had her skill, her enthusiasm, her Mascaro Tonique, and her space. She spent every waking moment planning the salon. Let's see, she mused. I need to make this shop a place where customers feel totally comfortable and delighted, just like I learned to please my employers. I have to find a way to wash their hair without the water and soapsuds running down the front of their faces and blouses.

"Aha! I know what will work," Martha exclaimed aloud. "I need a chair that will go backwards and a sink bowl that will fit the neck of the customers. A reclining shampoo chair is what I will call it! And a Harper bowl! All my inventions! Yippee!" She couldn't get the smile off her face.

But reality sometimes has a way of dashing hopes. With less than $360 in lifetime savings to rent the shop, buy products, and now these necessities, Martha started to worry. "I must find someone who can make these items for me cheaply." She asked Mrs. Roberts, but her boss had no idea. Then Mr. Roberts gave her the name of a German craftsman, an immigrant who had done some work on their mansion.

Hans looked at Martha's drawings and just stared and stared. After ten minutes had passed, Martha wondered if he actually spoke English. Just when she was going to give up, Hans looked up and said, "Ja, I can do this. Give me a week."

Martha replied, "My shop needs to open in two weeks; I need it sooner."

"Come back tomorrow," he told her.

The next day, Martha took the trolley to South Avenue and knocked on Hans's door. "Ja? Come in," Hans said. "Look." There in the middle of his parlor, with five children jumping up and down, was a reclining chair with sleigh-like feet, and yes, it tilted backwards.

Martha was so excited she asked if she could try it out. Then each of his children asked to try it out, and they all declared, "Sehr gut." Martha nodded in agreement. Ultimately, the chair became white, with cane backing and a more delicate footing, matching the white bowl with the neck indentation.

Hans even delivered and installed the chair and bowl. "Danke, danke," Martha replied when he was done.

Now all Martha lacked were customers. When a photographer asked to take a picture of her and her long, floor-length hair, Martha agreed—under the condition that she receive a copy of the picture. That photograph became Martha's advertisement. She pasted it on the glass window of her shop's door. She wanted people passing by to notice it and inquire about her services. That's exactly what they did. Her first patron was an artist from an office nearby.

High-society women were a little slower to come to Martha's salon. They still wanted her to come to their homes to dress their hair. Martha refused. Meanwhile, showman P.T. Barnum offered her (and her hair) $75 a week to appear in his circus. Martha refused him, too. She had faith in herself and her idea. Martha bided her time, and finally her business caught on because of another neighbor.

It was a music teacher who finally turned the tide. He moved in next door—without space for a waiting room. When Martha saw the mothers of his students standing outside in the hall, she cannily offered her space for them to wait. "Ladies, please, come and rest your weary feet in my salon. I have plenty of room." Soon the mothers of his pupils were having Martha do their hair, while the music lessons went on. Each of those women brought other women, and soon her shop was overwhelmed with society ladies.

Chapter 10

A Spa Experience

Martha walked briskly through the door of her salon in Room 516 of the Powers Building. Even after a year in business, Martha still got a thrill when she turned the door handle. She couldn't believe how her world had changed. Business had been so good that she had to hire an assistant. Thinking about who that might be, Martha reminded herself of her own history. I can hire a former servant just like me. We know how to please customers, and together we can change our world. Just imagine, someday I might have a whole room full of poor women eager to please our customers. She giggled to herself.

Martha's first assistant, Bertha Farquhar, worked for a friend of Mrs. Roberts. Thankfully, like the Roberts, Bertha's employer was supportive, and encouraged Bertha to try the new opportunity. When she first interviewed Bertha, Martha noticed that Bertha always looked down and barely spoke above a whisper.

"Bertha, we are businesswomen now. You need to be as kind and thoughtful as you always were while keeping house for the Browns, but in this shop, you are here as an equal. You must greet people warmly, but you also must speak clearly and look at them. Make them comfortable with your eyes and smile. Your hands will do the rest. Let them feel the blood vessels and make them flow. Wake up those sleeping cells. Let each customer delight in your every touch. Follow my EXACT directions about washing hair. Remember, no water is to splash on any customer. Your hands must be in control!

"Now, make sure the customer is comfortable before you place her neck into the cut-out of the sink. Then warm the water and wet the hair down. Apply my special shampoo and rub it in with your fingers, firmly stimulating the scalp. Use the palms of your hands to forcefully, but gently, massage the head three times, then move down to the neck and shoulders, and finally back to the head one more time with the pummeling of your hand.

"Next you apply the tonique, my secret formula, kneading it into the scalp. You will find there are no knots. Then brush the hair with my special boar-bristle brush for more stimulation."

"But, I thought you said we were washing hair. Why are we exercising the shoulders?" Bertha asked more boldly.

"Bertha, we begin at the shoulders and work our hands around. Remember, our goal is bringing out the inner beauty in everyone. That comes when we relax the body. Everything is connected. Blood flow leads to health. Slowly, but steadfastly, your hands go to work, Bertha," Martha explained, echoing her mentor, Dr. Herriman.

It took much practice. Bertha tried to follow Martha's detailed instructions. The final test was washing Martha's floor-length hair! Bertha seemed reluctant to brush firmly. "Blood flow, Bertha, remember," Martha explained. Bertha got bolder. Martha concluded that she was ready to start working.

On Bertha's first day, she met Martha outside the shop. "Good morning, Bertha. It's going to be a good day. I can just feel it." Martha found that if she started the day on a positive note, it usually ended that way as well.

"Good morning, Miss Harper. Would you like me to start by cleaning?"

"Bertha, in front of others, we will be formal, but between ourselves my name is Martha. I am your employer, but we are partners in the shop's success," she explained. "Now, I need to tell you about cleaning here, Bertha. Please remember to clean underneath the edges and the corners of the carpet."

"Really? Beneath the edges?"

"Bertha, you know we have a lot of fussy customers, and if they see dirt, they will think we don't do our work right."

"Yes, Miss Harper. Oops! Martha," Bertha giggled.

Martha smiled in response. Martha was trying to be an understanding boss. "Do it now, and then we'll both put on our aprons. Our first customer will be arriving soon."

Both women were already wearing clean white uniforms. They finished tying their white aprons and pinning on their white hats just as Mrs. Sibley came through the door. Mrs. Sibley was the wife of Rufus Sibley, who was an owner of the largest department store in Rochester. Bertha ran over to meet her as she'd been taught. "Good morning, Mrs. Sibley. Let me take your coat. Isn't it a lovely sunny day today? We don't always get sun in Rochester, so it is to be enjoyed."

"Sunny, yes, but that wind went right through me."

"Well, you sit down right here, Mrs. Sibley, and we'll see that you get all warmed up." Bertha quietly shook out a clean cape and put it around Mrs. Sibley's neck. Then she stepped away, as Martha vigorously washed her hands. "Mrs. Sibley, do you want a skin treatment today?" Martha inquired. Mrs. Sibley sighed. "Oh, yes, I understand it makes one look years younger."

Martha replied, "It makes your inner spirit come out and beam. Now to the shampoo chair." Martha took

Mrs. Sibley's hand, gently pulled her up, and guided her over to the special reclining chair.

"I can't get over this chair, Miss Harper. Wherever did you find it?"

Martha lowered the chair's rattan back and cradled her customer's neck in the marble sink with the special cut-out. "I didn't find it. I designed it and had it made. There's not another chair like it in Rochester. Nor another sink with a cut-out like this one either."

"Mrs. Lindsay told me about it, but I had to come and see it for myself. Just think. No more soap in my eyes. Someone should have invented this years ago."

Martha began the hour-and-a-half procedure— cleaning the skin, stimulating the skin, massaging it, and of course, working through the shoulders and neck, upward. Her hands moved in circular motions, from the heart upwards and around. Meanwhile, Mrs. Sibley snored away, totally relaxed.

When it was over, Bertha gushed, "You look beautiful, Mrs. Sibley."

"Thank you, Bertha, Please schedule me for another treatment in two weeks," Mrs. Sibley directed, as she paid Martha and gave her something extra as a thank you.

"Martha, I can't wait for my out-of-town guests to experience your shop. You make Rochester—and me— look so chic," she exclaimed as she waved goodbye and left.

Did the salon ever attract the kind of women that Mr. Powers had been afraid of? There were some. One day, Martha and Bertha rolled their eyes at each other when a woman who Mr. Powers would have called a trollop walked in.

"Good day, Miss Harper. I'm here for a hair wash and scalp treatment. I've heard about your services and want to try them out for myself."

"Bertha, go get a cape for …," she hesitated.

"Miss Smith," said the woman through bright red lips.

"Let me take your coat, Miss Smith."

Bertha tried not to look at the black lace daringly displayed below Miss Smith's skirt, which was shockingly high above the ankles. But she could not help noticing the woman's deep cleavage as she wrapped the cape around her shoulders.

Martha worked with unusual speed. When she was finished, Bertha had Miss Smith's coat waiting, and Martha walked her to the door.

"But you haven't told me what I owe you," said Miss Smith. She pulled some dollar bills out of her satin purse.

"Today's treatment is on the house," Martha said pleasantly, "but please don't return."

Miss Smith stuffed the money back in her purse, lifted her chin, and sashayed out the door. "Good day."

Martha closed the door behind her and turned to Bertha with a sigh. "That's that." With Miss Smith's footsteps fading down the hall, Martha and Bertha looked at each other again and started to laugh.

By this time, Bertha and Martha had become friends, and Bertha called her "Mattie," like her other close friends did. As they were closing the shop for the day, Bertha asked, "Mattie, have you have thought about marrying?"

"Sort of. I wouldn't consider it. Men control you in marriage. My mother was without any power to protect her children from being sent into servitude. Mrs. Roberts is chained to Mr. Roberts, whatever his misbehavior. My business and my home would become my husband's possessions. I will not be a servant again! No, we need Susan B. Anthony and the suffrage movement to win a lot more battles before a woman would ever be a man's equal in marriage," Martha concluded.

"Oh, my, Mattie, I never thought of those practical ideas. I just think it might be nice to have a romance," Bertha shared quietly.

"Sometimes you have to make choices in life, Bertha, but my choice does not have to be yours."

Chapter 11

Success

Mrs. Sibley was only one of the many socially-prominent women who patronized Martha's salon. Mrs. Strong, Mrs. Bausch, Mrs. Lomb, the VanVoorhis family – they all came and brought their friends. This was Martha's desired clientele. They had the money to spend on hair care and products, and Martha was very comfortable serving these women. She knew just how to pamper them, while promoting her method and her products. From her wealthy aunts to Mrs. Roberts and her friends, Martha had been serving women like this her whole life.

Martha also drew business from suffragists. Susan B. Anthony, who wore her silver hair in a bun, liked Martha's emphasis on health over beauty. She became Martha's customer and ardent supporter, describing her as a woman who was controlling her own destiny. "Every woman needs her own pocketbook," Anthony would lecture from the platforms, citing Harper as an example of what women could do. In fact, Harper and Anthony spent many hours after the shop closed talking about issues important to women. It wasn't by accident that Martha became the first woman to join the Rochester Chamber of Commerce.

Another suffragist, Mrs. Josephine Sargent Force, told everyone who would listen that she first tried the Harper Method because she was brought up a suffragist and interested in anything women were doing. Once she tried the method, she was hooked. Not only did she return for more treatments but also brought her friends.

After a while, Martha was so busy that she had to hire more assistants. Martha looked for women who had been domestic servants like herself. She knew that these women would have been trained to please customers, and pleasing customers was Martha's number one business practice. Only satisfied customers would recommend her shop to other women and help her business grow. Not only that, but Martha also wanted to help these former servants build a life and career of their own, as she had. And Martha certainly did not neglect her own family when looking for assistants. One of them was her own sister, Harriet, who also had been hired out as a servant by her parents.

Eventually, Martha's business was too big to fit in the one room she had at the Powers Building, and she went to see her landlord about renting more space.

"Mr. Powers, I'm afraid that I have a problem with my space."

"Oh? What's wrong? I'm sure that we can take care of any problem. Is it the heat, or the gas lights?"

"No. The heat is just fine. So are the lights. The problem, Mr. Powers, is that my business has become so successful that I'm running out of room. I need more space. I must add at least one more sink and two more massage stations. That is, if you're not afraid of me drawing the wrong clientele."

"Of course not, Miss Harper, of course not," he blustered. "You know, you're in luck. The space right next to you should be freeing up soon. I think it will be just the amount of space you need. I'll have my assistant draw up a lease for you to sign as soon as the other renter has moved out. What would you like? One year? Two?"

"Mr. Powers, Sir, I won't be signing any lease. You may figure out what the extra rent will be, and if it's agreeable to me, we'll continue on, month-to-month just as we have been doing."

"I see, Miss Harper. I see. Just as you wish. We'll continue on month-to-month."

Martha couldn't help reminding Mr. Powers about HER terms. She got her larger space and continued to run her business following the principles of Christian Science.

Sometimes that meant that Martha was in opposition to the latest hair trends. One day Bertha pulled Martha aside and whispered, "Mrs. Edmunds is asking me about hair dye. What should I say?"

"I'll handle this, Bertha."

Martha motioned Bertha to switch places with her, and she started to massage Mrs. Edmunds's scalp. "Mrs. Edmunds, your hair is so beautiful. Did you inherit this lovely color from your mother? It's most unusual. You know, some women actually want to dye their hair. Can you imagine covering up a color as unique as yours? Besides that, dying the hair involves the use of toxic chemicals. It's against the well-ordered plan of nature. All of my products contain natural ingredients. I just couldn't live with myself if I covered up a woman's natural beauty with chemicals. Could you?"

There was no more talk of hair dye from Mrs. Edmunds.

Demand for Martha's services grew and grew. What woman didn't want to believe that Martha was simply bringing out her own natural beauty using organic herbs and compounds? The best part was that Martha believed it herself. She continued to convince women that beauty came from good health, good healthy products, and good care. Martha's shop soon became a place where women brought their out-of-town friends when they were visiting. Martha's name became known even outside of Rochester. How could life get any better than this?

Chapter 12

Franchising

Martha's out-of-town visitors were soon clamoring for Martha to open shops in their hometowns.

"I'd love to have a salon like this in Buffalo," said Mrs. Charles Bishop, the mayor's wife.

"But, we so treasure your patronage here, Mrs. Bishop," replied Martha.

"Yes, but, Miss Harper, I can't always get over here to Rochester. How I'd love to get a facial more often."

Mrs. Bishop was not the first woman to request a shop in her home city. Martha had been thinking over how to expand and had an answer for Mrs. Bishop when she pressed her about it. "Mrs. Bishop, I'd gladly open a salon in Buffalo if you could guarantee me customers."

"I know many women who would love to come to your salon for treatments. No one gives a scalp massage like you and your girls do, Miss Harper."

"I so appreciate the compliment, Mrs. Bishop, but I can't build a business on wishes and promises. I'll tell you what, if you can bring me a petition with the signatures of women who are committed to using a Harper Salon, I'll consider coming to Buffalo and opening one."

That is also exactly what she told Mrs. Bertha Palmer, the queen of Chicago society, who was introduced to the Rochester salon by her friend, Mrs. Grace Coolidge, the future First Lady. Mrs. Coolidge was introduced to the Harper Method by Mrs. Alexander Graham Bell after a visit to the Rochester School for the Deaf.   It was women's networking in full force, and everyone clamored for a Harper experience.

"Martha, you must commit to opening a salon in time for the Chicago World's Fair in 1893. The world will be visiting, and I am in charge of the Women's Pavilion. I want the Harper Method to be part of Chicago's showcase," declared Bertha Palmer.

"Thank you so much, Mrs. Palmer, but first I need a petition from twenty-five of your best friends, assuring me that they will have a treatment at my shop IF I come," Martha instantly replied.   Only after she uttered this declaration, did she think: who am I to demand anything from such a woman? Then Martha smiled to herself. You are Martha Matilda Harper, and they want you and your method!

Both Mrs. Bishop and Mrs. Palmer followed through on getting the pledges, and just three years after opening her Rochester salon, Martha opened her first "branch office" in Buffalo. In keeping with her values of helping family and helping other servants like herself, Martha gave her sister, Harriet, the opportunity to be the shop owner.

Buffalo was one thing, but Chicago was something else again. Buffalo was only sixty miles from Rochester, but Chicago was over six hundred miles away. What should she do? Susan B. Anthony encouraged Martha to set up the satellite in Chicago. The World's Fair would be bringing people from all over the world, and Martha would be a role model for other women to copy. But, how could she structure the business so she could expand without sacrificing quality? How could she help other poor women, yet thrive herself? The banks were unlikely sources for loans. Maybe her female, wealthy customers might be supportive, Martha thought to herself.

That's when Martha got the idea to model her business after the Christian Science structure, with its strong Mother Church (headquarters), and its satellite operations (churches), its strict operations manual of how leadership would be established and what prayers would be read when.

Martha thought—I can duplicate that. Rochester will be headquarters. I will write a manual detailing how to do the various procedures and how to run a shop. I will bring the Harperites back for training in Rochester and social support. I will visit them to assure all is running properly. They will buy and use only my products, including the chair and bowl, along with my hair and skin care line. Shop owners will pay me back from their earnings. As she vowed to Bertha and Harriet, "We will succeed together!"

In 1893, Mrs. Reynolds, a Harper trainee and former servant girl, went to Chicago with Martha's backing to become a businesswoman herself. After a promising start, things almost fell apart. Mrs. Reynolds fell ill with a gall bladder attack and ended up in the hospital.

Martha immediately asked Bertha, her trusted first hire, to go to Chicago to take over. Bertha was only twenty-four and had never been outside of Rochester. Besides that, she was suffering from a broken heart. It was only her loyalty and gratitude to Martha that gave her the courage to go. "I've never been a foot outside of Rochester, and now you want me to travel all by myself, Mattie?" Bertha moaned.

"Bertha, trust me, this will change your life. You will now become an owner. You will have my total backing, my products, and my methods. I will choose the location. I will bring you back for training, but only if you can properly handle Mrs. Palmer and her friends. Think of the potential—a fresh start. I will never desert you like your boyfriend did," Martha consoled Bertha, who was shaking.

Mrs. Reynolds ended up coming home for good. She didn't want to be so far away from home if her gall bladder acted up again. Bertha got the shop open in time for the fair, and it was a roaring success. On the fairgrounds, people from all over the world were sampling for the first time Pabst Blue Ribbon beer, Cream of Wheat cereal, Juicy Fruit gum, and Cracker Jack popcorn. At the Chicago Harper Salon, they could experience the Harper Method and Mascaro Tonique for the first time. Martha was in good company.

After the fair, Bertha relocated that shop to Chicago's prestigious Marshall Field's building and department store. Similarly, Rachel Stothart opened a shop in Detroit in 1891. Salons in Pittsburgh, Boston, St Paul, Spokane, New York City, Santa Barbara, and San Francisco soon followed. It wasn't long before Harper Salons spanned the whole United States and Canada— even Europe, the Caribbean, and eventually Asia and South America. Martha and the Harper Method were gaining attention everywhere.

Martha's unique business model became known as the "franchise" system. She launched the first retail franchise in America. Little did Martha know that the word franchising comes from the French word, which means "to free from servitude." That is, however, exactly what Martha did. The first one hundred of her five hundred shops all went to impoverished women. Martha was the franchisor, and each new shop owner was a franchisee. The franchisor and franchisee were strongly tied to each other. Each had a brighter future because of the other. Martha had invented a new way of doing business.

Martha did not have time to sit back and savor the benefits of success. In fact, with the establishment of each new franchise, Martha's work increased. She knew that her success depended on the success of her franchisees. She didn't want to succeed at the expense of others, but, rather, she wanted to elevate other women to be successful alongside her. Building success took hard work.

The first step was training. Martha started training the franchisees in her own salon. They worked as shop assistants, learning by observing and then doing. Martha taught her girls more than just the practical skills of hair care and massage. She had already chosen her pupils on the basis of their abilities to serve others, but she made sure that they modeled exemplary behavior and a gentle, calm manner. Again, Christian Science practices were carrying over into her business practices. She emphasized trust, kindness, cooperation, teamwork, and mutual support. She cautioned them against gossiping and taught them to lead by example, as she did herself.

Martha followed up the training program with visits to the new salons to ensure that her products and methods were being implemented correctly. As years went on, Martha found more ways to connect with franchisees, but not before dealing with some problems at home.

Chapter 13

Problems at Home

Martha and the Roberts had become like family. Although the Roberts were warmer and kinder than her own parents had been, eventually other problems arose. They had encouraged her to start manufacturing her Tonique in their shed and to start up a business, but as Martha's success grew, theirs declined. As Martha was preparing to open the Detroit shop in 1891, she confided in her trusted assistant, Rachel.

"Come, sit with me, Rachel, and share a pot of tea. This business with the Roberts has me upset. I need to talk about it, but you have to keep what I say just between us."

"Of course, Mattie, you know I'd never betray a confidence."

Martha patted her assistant's hand. "I know, Rachel. That's why I am trusting you with the Detroit shop. Now, let's see …" She stirred some honey into her tea. "I don't quite know where to begin." The steam rose from her cup, and she took a sip. Rachel leaned in, sipping her own beverage.

"I suppose it started with Mr. Roberts losing $30,000 in that Staten Island real estate deal."

Rachel drew in a breath. "Thirty thousand dollars? Oh, my, I never knew anyone who had that much money."

"That's only the beginning. He's lost more in other bad investments. I've had to pay $1,500 in interest so that they don't lose the house."

"Oh, my!" Rachel's eyes got bigger. She set her cup down. "What next?"

"I've had to take over paying the bills and the taxes. You know that Mrs. Roberts is too ill to do anything, and now we have her hospital bills as well, poor thing." Martha took a long drink from her cup and kept talking. "That's not the worst of it. Mr. Roberts is drinking more heavily than ever. Last night he and his friend, Seward French, got so drunk that I had to have Mr. French physically removed from the house."

Rachel gasped.

"All night long they were pestering me to sign some legal papers. Mr. Roberts wants me to turn over a part of my business to him."

"What will you do?"

"Well, I can't leave them. I can't desert Mrs. Roberts when she needs me, and I can't leave her alone with that drunk of a husband. I don't mind helping them financially, but I'm not going to turn over any part of my business. That's where I draw the line. I've worked so hard to have a business of my own. I'm not going to work hard just to turn over my earnings to him—like I had to do with my own father."

"Good for you, Mattie. That's why all the girls admire you so much. We want to be successful like you."

"You will, dear." She patted Rachel's hand again. "You will." She drank the last of her tea. "Thanks for listening, Rachel. You're a dear."

"Think nothing of it, Mattie. And I won't tell a soul. I promise." She took the cup from Martha's hand. "Here, let me clean up. You go home and rest."

"I'll go home, but I don't know about resting."

Chapter 14

Romance

As soon as her business got on its feet, Martha followed Mr. VanVoorhis' suggestion and hired a private tutor to make up for her lack of formal education. She spent what little free time she had studying. Martha wanted to be treated as an equal by the businessmen of the community, and she didn't want to give anyone an excuse to put her down. Martha studied literature, history, psychology, physiology, and fine arts. She also took extension courses at the University of Rochester, which at the time was located on University Avenue, just behind her home.

Martha had no time for marriage and a family of her own. She did not trust men and the power they had to impact lives, like her mother's or Mrs. Roberts'. The laws were stacked against women, and a person was freer if she could control her own life. Instead, the Roberts and the girls in her shops became her family. The business was her child.

The year 1901 marked the beginning of a new century, and Martha looked to the future with optimism. The Harper Method continued to grow—even as the Roberts's finances got worse. The year 1901 also marked the year that the Roberts were forced to declare bankruptcy.

Martha continued to open new shops around America and the world. In 1908, in the midst of opening a new salon in Cincinnati, Ohio, and preparing for a future shop in Berlin, Germany, Martha took some time out for some unfinished family business. Martha made a pilgrimage to the Oakville Cemetery, Oakville, Ontario, where her mother had been buried in 1885. While there, she arranged for a new sizable tombstone to be laid in honor of Beady and Martha's siblings, Nellie and James, who had died as infants. Beady Harper, who never got any acknowledgment in life, who had died at the age of fifty-one, after bearing ten children and having to give them all away, finally had her tribute.

Martha's sisters, Emma and Harriet, clung to Martha for support as they stood admiring the new stone. "I couldn't do anything to help you, Mother, but I swear I'll help my sisters, and other women too, to have a better life," said Martha.

Martha gave no such tribute to her father. In fact, there is no record of Robert Harper's burial. His epithet was provided by his great-granddaughter, Catherine O'Leary, who pronounced him "the man who gave away all his children." Although Martha didn't invent the phrase, "Living well is the best revenge," she surely thought it.

By 1909, the business was doing so well that Martha hired John Bushfield, a graduate of Oberlin College and a chemist, to manage the production of the tonic and other products. That would allow Martha to focus on marketing and motivating, opening new franchises and training the franchisees. She seemed to have a sixth sense of where to locate. As Mina from Detroit said, "She knows the street we should be in, even the building. Let a flood wipe out downtown, she knows where to put us and how to get a great deal on the space."

Finally, in 1912, with the new manager on board, Martha decided to take a real vacation. She was fifty-five years old. Martha called on her friends and salon owners to go with her. "Girls, I've got exciting plans. Who wants to go with me on a vacation?"

"Where are you going, Mattie? You've already been to Europe."

"Yes, Bertha, but that was for business. Berlin, London, and Paris were great; wasn't it something when the Kaiser bowed to ME as he passed in the parade in Germany? Now I want to do something just for fun."

"What could be more fun than Paris?"

"What about a trip out West? I've been reading about a tour of Yellowstone, our first national park."

"How would we get there, on horseback?"

"That's very funny, Rachel. We'll take the train, of course. The Northern Pacific Railroad will take us to Gardiner, Montana, and from there we'll get a stagecoach into the park."

"Are you sure you don't want to open a new salon in the park?" asked Bertha.

"Yes, I've heard that bears love facials," added Rachel.

Bertha laughed. "That does sound like fun, but how much will it cost?"

"It will cost $40 per person, but that includes all of our transportation, lodging, and meals."

"Forty dollars? That's two week's salary for some people."

"Yes, Bertha, but we're all wealthy shop owners, remember?"

Everyone laughed again. "In that case, I'm buying new clothes for the trip," said Bertha.

As usual, Martha's enthusiasm was contagious, and the group set out for adventure. Little did Martha know that this trip would change her life.

Once in Yellowstone, Martha and her friends hired a stagecoach driver and guide named Robert Arthur MacBain. Unlike the other guides who looked like cowboys, Robert looked and acted more like an underfed city slicker. He was a science teacher using his summer vacation to find a new career.

Robert knew how to treat a lady. He was charming, polite, and respectful, taking their hands as they alit from the coach in their new linen dusters and hats and guiding them to the paths. Did he linger a little longer in holding Martha's hand? The girls thought so, teasing Martha about her new boyfriend. Martha told them it was just because she was the shortest and needed the most help that Robert paid her more attention, but she couldn't deny that it was to her that he offered his arm as they made their way up the paths to Rustic Falls and Swan Lake Flat, to Obsidian Cliff and Frying Pan Flats. Every time Robert would hold out his arm, the girls would giggle and Martha would blush. She hoped he didn't notice.

Robert was a college-educated man who loved to tell stories. "Have you heard about the day that Teddy Roosevelt was walking right over there when a bear came strolling out of the woods?" Each story began with "Have you heard?" and ended with a laugh. He had a gift for mimicry and could imitate everyone from the former president to the bear, itself. The girls agreed that they hadn't laughed so much in a long time.

The last night of the trip was magical. Martha's friends all insisted that they were extremely tired and needed to retire early when Robert suggested a moonlit stroll along the Old Faithful boardwalk. "What about you,

Miss Harper? You're not too tired, are you? You must see the geyser by moonlight."

"It would be rude to turn down your generous offer when you must be tired yourself, Mr. MacBain." Martha didn't know how to feel when they took off arm in arm. Other men had given her their attention, but Martha was never interested. This man and this time were different. He was not overpowering, but respectful. Even his stature was perfect. At 5'8", he was shorter than many men, but taller than Martha, who stood less than five feet. Yet his slim body did not dominate.

"It will be so hard to leave here tomorrow morning, Mr. MacBain. I shall miss these mountains, the geysers, the waterfalls and the hot springs, all with such enchanting names."

"Speaking of enchanting names—I think your name is enchanting, Miss Harper. May I take the liberty of calling you Martha?"

"Only if you'll allow me to call you Robert."

"Robert and Martha it is."

"Forgive me, Robert, but when will we again have a chance to address each other as such? I'm leaving tomorrow, and Rochester, New York, is a long way from Yellowstone Park and also from your home in Iowa."

"They do have mail service in Rochester, don't they? That is if you would be so kind as to allow me to correspond with you?"

"Why, Robert, I'd be delighted to hear from you. Promise me you'll include one of your stories in your letter."

"I shall, my dear. I shall." He kissed her gloved hand.

"Here, Robert." She took off the glove and handed it to him. "This will be a remembrance of our time together."

Robert bent down and picked up a pine cone. "And this will be a remembrance that I am here pining for you."

"Oh, Robert." Martha didn't sleep all night and never once thought about the business.

The business had always been Martha's child, and when she got home, she found that it demanded her attention all the more for being away. There were new girls waiting to be trained in the Harper Method and new sites to be considered for future franchisees.

Martha thought about Robert and found herself checking the mail every day for a letter. As the days wore on, though, she was afraid that their time together had all been a dream—a sweet dream, but a dream nonetheless. She was a businesswoman, not some poor girl who deluded herself that she needed a man to be happy. And why would Robert write to her when she was twenty-four years older than he—although she certainly had not revealed that to him.

But Robert was true to his word, and the first letter from him arrived within several weeks. "Dearest Martha," it began. "A terrible thing has happened here at Yellowstone. The hot springs have lost all their steam. The geysers have lost their energy. The rainbow colors have dimmed—all because you are not here." It continued on about his activities and ended with a story that made her laugh out loud. Wait until I tell the girls, she thought.

So began their long distance relationship. They learned about each other through their letters and found that they had much in common. Although Robert had more formal education than Martha, his background was like Martha's in that he had an unhappy childhood. The youngest of nine children working in an Iowa farm family, Robert had always felt different from the rest. He was the only one of his farm family who valued "book learning" above working on the land. He, too, wanted to escape his destiny. He did not want to be a farmer. His parents, he wrote, were like Martha's father in that they could be very cruel.

Soon Martha and Robert became "Mattie" and "Robbie." When Robbie wrote that he was thinking of attending Columbia Law School in New York City, Mattie dropped the letter in excitement. When Robbie headed east, suddenly their 2,000 mile separation was reduced to 350 miles, and Martha found more and more reasons to make the trip from Rochester to New York City, opening many shops there and in the nearby suburbs of New Jersey and Connecticut.

Mattie and Robbie continued to grow closer, and eventually even the shorter distance became too much. It was Martha who made the next move. "Robbie," Martha wrote, "we make a good team. You are ever so bright and clever. I have this growing business that needs help. Why don't we team up?"

Robert felt grateful to Martha and knew she offered him a path out of Iowa farm life. Yet, he wondered what role a man could play in Martha's business, let alone her life. In 1916, after four years of letters and trips back and forth, Robert agreed to come to Rochester as Martha's executive assistant. But circumstances would soon interfere with Martha's plans again.

Chapter 15

War Correspondence

World War I began in Europe in 1914. By 1917, America had joined the battle, and Robert enlisted in the U. S. Army in May of that year. Once again Mattie and Robbie were forced into a long-distance relationship. Once again the letters flew back and forth. Camped in the war-torn fields of Europe, Robert, wrote, "Martha, although this is an awful situation with people killing each other, in a strange way it makes me feel important. I love my job driving an ambulance. Although I've seen some awful things that people shouldn't have to see, my role helps people. I'm needed here, and I'm respected here. And from now on you may call me Captain MacBain."

Martha wasted no time in writing back. "Dear CAPTAIN MacBain, it comes as no surprise to me that you are needed and respected in Europe, because you have shown yourself to be needed and respected here in America and especially here in the Harper business. I would never try to take you away from doing your duty, and I admire you so for volunteering, but just know that you are missed."

While Robert was away, Martha was never at a loss for things to do. There were always new franchisees to train, new locations to scout out, and everyday budget matters to go over. As if that weren't enough, there were always the Roberts's problems to attend to.

Late one afternoon after an especially long and trying day, Martha was muttering under her breath as she pulled on her raincoat, "I hope the streetcar's not delayed by the rain." She had one hand on the doorknob when the door swung out forcefully, making her lose her balance. She fell into the arms of the building delivery man.

"Oh, Miss Harper, I'm sorry. I hope I didn't hurt you. This package just arrived for you, and I was anxious to catch you before you started for home."

Martha leaned against the door frame. "It's okay, Joe. Set it on the desk over there. I'll look at it tomorrow."

"Miss Harper, Ma'am. You might want to look at it tonight. It's from London, England."

Martha stood up straight, alert now. "Let me see it." With only one glance she could identify the handwriting. She plopped into the nearest chair and ripped off the wrapping paper while Joe lingered by the door.

"It's not often that a person gets a package all the way from London, England, is it Ma'am?"

"What? Oh, no it certainly isn't an everyday event is it?" She glanced over at Joe. "Oh, I'm sorry. Let me get you something for your trouble." Martha ran to her desk, dropped the half-open box and reached in the top drawer for some coins. "Here you go." She didn't wait for a reply as she closed the door behind him.

Martha couldn't open the box fast enough. Inside were the most beautiful books she had ever seen. Both were covered in soft brown leather with embossed gold letters. The first was titled *King James' Bible*. The second was Mary Baker Eddy's *Science and Health*. These were books that Martha knew well. She went to both of them for inspiration and courage to face each day. She dug back into the box to search for a card, and she wasn't disappointed. Tears welled in her eyes as she read it aloud.

"Dear Mattie, these are special copies of special books for someone very special to me. When I lay here at night with guns resounding around me, I shall think of you reading these books that I know you love, and I shall smile before I drop off to sleep." Martha just sat there a few minutes and let the tears flow. He gets me. He really gets me, she thought. For the first time in my life, I've found a man who understands me.

When Martha finally got up, her mood had totally shifted. The weariness was gone. She repacked the books carefully and strode with confidence and determination out to face the rain.

Robert stayed in France until August, 1919, and traveled with some of his army buddies, but he faithfully kept up the correspondence with Martha and also took the time to visit Harper salons in Europe.

As it turned out, Robert was not the only one visiting Harper salons in Europe. After the war, Martha delighted in telling this story. "During the negotiations of the Treaty of Versailles, President Woodrow Wilson found himself under terrible nervous strain. He was so nervously exhausted each evening that he could not sleep. His secretary arranged a private evening appointment for him in the Paris Harper Method Salon, and he was able to enjoy the relaxing massage, brushing, and Harper Method scalp preparations. He became so relaxed, completely losing his conference-created tension that he was able to sleep soundly. So impressed was the President, that he had Harper Method equipment installed in the White House."

Chapter 16

Marriage

Martha could now boast a president as one of her customers. At this point, she really needed help in running her ever-expanding business. The first person who came to mind was Robert, who returned to Rochester in 1920. Martha now had 175 franchisees. "Robbie, team up with me," she gently coaxed. "Help me build this Harper Empire. We need buildings and operational oversight. I need to keep my eye on motivating our team, finding new shop locations and the staff to fill them."

His response? "Oh, Mattie, I would do anything to help you." Robert once again became a Harper employee.

On a business trip to New York City in October, 1920, eight years after they had first met, Martha laid all her cards on the table. Coyly, she asked Robert to come to her hotel room to see her trousseau.

"Mattie, I didn't know you were thinking of marriage. Who is the lucky man?"

She winked at him and replied, "You are."

They lost no time in getting married, saying "I do" on October 27 in a small Greenwich Village church. Martha was sixty-three, Robert, thirty-nine. They honeymooned in Atlantic City, New Jersey. They were very, very happy—their families, especially Robert's, not so much.

When Robert brought Martha to Iowa to introduce her to the family, things did not go as Martha would have liked. "Mother," Robert said while placing one arm around Martha's waist, "I'd like you to meet Martha Matilda Harper, now Mrs. MacBain."

"I'm Mrs. MacBain," his mother said, and she turned her back on Martha to stir the pot on her stove before Martha could extend her hand in greeting.

Martha kept a smile on her face as she had first learned to do so long ago when serving her miserable aunts and grandmother. But Martha was not that scared little girl anymore. When Robert's niece, Esther, appeared, Martha gave her one dollar to buy something in town. Off Esther ran into town and came back having purchased several necklaces. Proudly she showed Martha what she had purchased, only to have Elspet, Robert's mother, grab them away. "These are cheap baubles, girl," she hissed.

Martha, without missing a beat, bent down and took off her necklace and put it around the crying girl's neck. "Esther, here is my necklace, and I assure you that it is not cheap!" Martha smiled her warm smile, and Esther smiled back.

Relations between Martha and the MacBains never became really cordial, especially with Robert's mother. Esther would report back that whenever Elspet spoke of Martha, she always hissed "that scientist."

Robert had some adjusting to do with Martha's family too. "Robbie, when you marry me, you marry my family. That means Mrs. Roberts always will live with us in our new home. Anyone from my family will always be welcome to stay with us, and my girls (the Harper staff and shop owners) will always be welcome, too."

"Of course," Robert responded. "I would have it no other way," but he coughed and looked away as he said that. Company gossips knew that Captain MacBain viewed Martha's family as moochers and that he never warmly embraced them. However, Robert was clever enough not to directly tell Martha his true feelings.

Nonetheless, Robert and Martha's marriage thrived. In marrying Robert, Martha not only gained a husband, but also American citizenship. By marrying Martha, Robert not only gained a wife, but also a thriving business that he could be part of. No more worries about being a farm boy. Now he could mingle with society people and discuss more than the price of hogs and corn.

And so they forged a life together. Their home became a Harper hotel. When out-of-town Harperites

105

came in for training or meetings, they were welcomed into the MacBain/Harper home. Robert seemed to thrive on being charming to the Harperites. He continued to be the attentive man about the house and the business. He insisted on being called "Captain," but it was Martha who actually steered the ship in the '20s and early '30s, with a bit of Robert's influence and preference.

It seemed that the only one who wasn't charmed by Robert was John Bushfield, Martha's first manager. Bushfield was so devoted to Martha that he named his son "John Harper Bushfield." However, he made a fateful mistake in refusing to call Robert "Captain." Ultimately Robert fired him. Martha, of course, backed her husband's decision. The company power was shifting, slowly.

Chapter 17

Competition

The Harper salons were not without competition. Martha faced a number of challenges over the many years she was in business—aside from the challenge of being accepted as a woman in business. Men began to notice the potential of the beauty industry for women. In 1897, a Frenchman named Marcel Grateau created a new curling iron that created a new beauty trend, the Marcel wave. Charles Revlon launched the Revlon business and suggested the beauty industry's goal had to be selling "hope in a jar."

As the Roaring Twenties hit America, women's clothing styles and hair styles were rapidly changing. The flapper style of short, fringed dresses and short, bobbed hair became very popular. Women were even coloring their hair. Not Martha. While she modified and expanded her skin care products and salon services, no hair dyes were ever allowed in her operation as long as she was CEO. She herself seemed to magically never gray and later admitted to using hennas! But dangerous chemicals were not allowed.

As Martha became more successful, she no longer needed her long, beautiful hair as a marketing tool. Although she did not "bob" her hair in the flapper style of the 1920s, she did start wearing her hair pinned up in back.

Martha also faced competition from others who created beauty products for women. Between 1890 and 1924, over 450 trademarks for women's beauty products were filed by women. Helena Rubenstein and Elizabeth Arden were two of Martha's biggest competitors, although both stressed make-up as a way toward outer beauty. Martha held to her view of inner beauty, although she packaged her products for sale in department stores and took out ads in ladies' magazines such as *Cosmopolitan, Vogue*, and *Ladies' Home Journal*.

In the 1920s, Martha faced competition from another direction—male barbers. Across the country, barbers were banding together in support of state laws that would prohibit women's hair salons from cutting hair. They wanted to make it necessary for everyone who cut hair to have a barber's license. Some states sided with barbers, and other states, including New York State, sided with hairdressers. The battle became fierce at times, and

Martha heard of a woman who was actually fined thirty days in the city workhouse for cutting hair without a license.

Martha managed to stay out of this battle and continued to run her business as she always had. She didn't criticize her competitors; she ignored them. Maybe for this reason, The Harper Method was snubbed by other beauty associations of its day. Martha was outraged by some of the things that she read.

"Listen to this, girls." Martha was reading aloud from the February, 1923 issue of *Burke's Beauty Journal*. "'The beauty culture is only in its first toddling steps of infancy.' How can they say that when there are over three hundred Harper Method shops worldwide?"

"You've shown them, Martha!"

"And look at this. Wilfred Academy in New York City has a big ad claiming to be America's first beauty school in 1918. By that time, I'd trained the staff of over one hundred salons."

"Shall we write them a letter, Martha?"

"No. Throw that magazine away. I'm just blowing off steam. We'll let our success speak for itself."

Chapter 18

A New Laboratory

Martha and the Harper Method were a success by anybody's standards, but success has its costs, and Martha and Robert found themselves still having to spend time apart. In the year since they'd married, the number of Harper salons had doubled from 75 to 150. While Martha traveled to recruit, inspire, and locate new shops, Robert managed the business and the manufacturing center at home. Robert was more to Martha than just a handsome, courteous escort. He actively participated in running the business and oversaw the construction of a new laboratory: a scientific, manufacturing laboratory, but also a learning laboratory.

On one of her visits home between business trips, Robert shared the plans of the new building with Martha. "Just look at this design, Mattie. These tanks will be made of glass-lined steel. We'll have steam-jacketed vats and a modern assembly line for washing, sterilizing and mixing."

"Oh, Robbie," Martha covered his hand with hers. "We've come such a long way from my first laboratory in the Roberts' garage and that cramped space in the Powers Building." She put on her reading glasses and looked more closely at the plans. "What are these lines around the top?"

"That's the catwalk, Mattie. Our men can walk around up there to control the outflow from the tanks into the mixing vats two stories below."

"Where will we keep the chemicals?"

"They'll be stored safely below ground."

"Why, Robbie, you've thought of everything." She gave him a big kiss.

"Wait 'til you see your own office. This will look like a proper business from the outside: brick and mortar for stability, lots of windows for enlightenment, and urns at the top for immortality."

Martha clapped her hands together. "I'm so glad I married a scholar." She thought for a minute. "Are you sure we can afford this?"

"We can't afford not to do it, Mattie. You know how many young women are clamoring to learn the Harper Method, and you've said yourself how cramped your space is in the Powers Building. Besides, why should we make Mr. Powers rich with our rent money? We'll invest in ourselves."

"Of course, you're right, Robbie." She looked at the floor. "If only I had gotten a patent for the reclining chair. Salons all over the world are using my design now. Think of the money I would have."

Robbie lifted Martha's chin with his left hand. "Look at me, Mattie. Thinking about 'if only' is a waste of time, and you've never wasted a minute of time in your life. The company has plenty of money and is making more every day."

"I know. You're right, Robbie. I just need you to encourage me from time to time." Martha looked at the drawing again. "How will people driving by know what this is? Will we have a sign?"

"Leave that to me, Mattie. Just leave that to me."

Construction got underway in the spring of 1921. Mattie loved seeing the progress every time she returned from a business trip. Meanwhile Robert took care of the details. He even planned a formal cornerstone ceremony for August 21, 1921, thirty-three years to the day that Martha's original Harper Hairdressing Parlor had opened.

Martha wasn't so keen on the ceremony. "Have it if you want, Robbie, but I don't think I need to be there. You're the one who's been here every day supervising this construction." The building site was at 1233 East Main Street, conveniently just down the street from their home, and they were walking over the property, checking on the day's progress.

"Why, Mattie, this business was started by you—and you alone. Who else could select the items for the cornerstone, and who else could explain their significance?"

"Okay, Robbie, if you really think so."

As Martha and Robert walked down Main Street on the day of the ceremony, they could see that a crowd was already gathering.

"Maybe this wasn't a good idea," said Martha.

"You can't back out now." Robert grabbed her arm more firmly. She had a brief memory of the first time that Robert had taken her arm in Yellowstone Park, but another glimpse of the crowd brought her back to reality.

"You didn't tell me you'd invited the mayor."

"I wanted to surprise you, my dear." Robert steered her toward the front of a makeshift stage. He nudged her forward.

Martha said a silent prayer of thanksgiving, and then welcomed the crowd. "I want to thank you all so much for coming." She looked over at her husband. "Robert didn't tell me that he had invited half of the city of Rochester." Laughter from the crowd made her more comfortable. She continued. "Let me try to explain to you, what this day means to me." She gave a quick overview of her early life and a more detailed outline of her early years in business.

"Now let me show you what I've brought for the cornerstone." She held up a few faded photographs.

114

"These are pictures of me and some of my early assistants: Bertha, Rachel, my sister Harriet." There was a ripple of polite applause. "And here is the first 50-cent piece I earned at the salon."

"Are you sure it's real?" came a cry from the crowd.

Martha laughed. "I'm sure it's real. I just don't know whether I want to bury it or spend it," she retorted. "I have just a few things more. Here are the copies of the Harper patent and product labels," She paused, "and now the most important things." Martha held up her Bible and the copy of Mary Baker Eddy's *Science and Health* that Robert had given her—the treasured leather-bound set that he had sent her from Europe during the war, the set she cherished so much. Robert dabbed at his eyes with a white handkerchief he pulled from his upper jacket pocket. "Yes, I had a surprise for you, too, Robert."

When the applause died down, Martha spoke again. "We have laid a foundation today, not of stone, mortar, brick, or any other material substance. We have laid a spiritual foundation upon which, during my whole lifetime, I have tried to build the Harper Method. It was founded on Principle and Truth, and it succeeded only because it had such a foundation." Martha motioned Robert forward, grabbed his arm, and they both took a bow. The laboratory was officially dedicated.

When the laboratory was complete in May, 1922, Mattie and Robbie marveled at what they had accomplished. Robert had provided the know-how to build the structure, but Martha had built the worldwide network of shops to need the products. They were quite the team. Robert MacBain, the farmer's son from Iowa, now oversaw a business empire. Martha, the servant girl from Munn's Corners had provided the means for hundreds of other poor girls to escape servitude.

Whenever Martha looked at the new laboratory, she couldn't help but think back to Dr. Herriman and das Labor. She and Robbie had laughed many times about how she had stolen into the Labor and broken the bottle, about how fearful she had been that she would be fired. If only Dr. Herriman could be here right now, she thought, and witness the three words carved in concrete above the center window of this laboratory:

MARTHA MATILDA HARPER

Chapter 19

Sharing Good News

With the headquarters completed, Martha undertook a new project. In 1923, she started a company newsletter called *Harper Method Progress*. It became a way of providing support and continuing education for all of the branch salon owners, the franchisees. Everyone would be receiving the same information at the same time. This was especially important because of their exclusion from the rest of the beauty product community. But that was not all. Mostly, Martha wanted to maintain the sense of family that had always characterized her relationships with shop owners. She encouraged all her Harperites to share both business and personal news so that they could be mutually helpful and happy.

Each newsletter included an advice column from Martha that began, "Dear Girls." She was a mother writing to her children.

In June 1926, Martha wrote in *Harper Method Progress*, "… The great Achievement of the Harper Method does not consist of the large number of our shops—though the sun never sets on them. It is not counted by the daily dollars our cash registers record. It does not rest on the scientific perfection of our treatments and our formulae, or wholly in the service we give. The Great Achievement of the Harper Method is the women it has made."

Although the newsletter served its purpose and provided a connection between shop owners who were literally spread around the world, Martha thrived on an even more personal connection. She arranged for summer "refresher" courses to be taught in Rochester to her franchisees. This was one more way of assuring that her product maintained consistency throughout all the franchises. She called the events "Reunions."

When out-of-town Harperites came in for training, they were welcome to stay in the Harper/MacBain home. In May, 1925, Martha and Robert, along with Mrs. Roberts, moved to a mansion at 853 Culver Road. It had been the former mayor's home. The whole top floor was a dormitory where Martha's special girls stayed when they came to town.

Martha never apologized for her wealth, although she remained approachable and down-to-earth. She often rode the trolley just like her employees. But this "girl" who started life as a servant, now had servants of her own: cook, chauffeur, and housekeeper. Dinner was presented in silver-covered serving dishes, and guests were provided with finger bowls. Visitors were tickled to find a telephone hidden as a bird feeder in the garden.

Money alone does not convey social status, but Mr. and Mrs. Robert MacBain were warmly accepted into Rochester society. By 1931, they were listed in Rochester's *Blue Book*, the Who's Who of Rochester society. They were members of the prestigious Oak Hill Country Club where Martha played golf. Martha also held membership in the Women's City Club, the Memorial Art Gallery, the Eastern Star, the Rochester Historical Society, and the American Legion Auxiliary. George Eastman included the MacBains in the Sunday soirees at his East Avenue mansion.

They sponsored a variety of New York State Democratic Women's events at their mansion and hosted governors there, also.

Along with high society members, Martha could claim presidents and first ladies among her clientele. Both President and Mrs. Coolidge were devoted to the Harper Method. In fact, when Martha came to Washington, D.C., Mrs. Coolidge filled her hotel room with flowers. More importantly, Mrs. Coolidge told her friends about the

Harper method, and Martha's customer list expanded to include many government leaders. Eventually, the Kennedy clan and then Lady Bird Johnson became devoted customers, too.

Chapter 20

Harper Method Textbook

Not only was the number of Harper salons increasing, but the number of training schools increased, too. Ultimately, Martha would have four more training schools: in Atlanta, Georgia, and Madison, Wisconsin, in the United States, and Winnipeg and Vancouver in Canada. In order to standardize training at all the schools, she wrote a training manual, *Harper Method Textbook*, published in 1926.

The textbook was very thorough. It was comprised of 216 pages, organized into 61 chapters, with blank pages included for notes. The book started with a statement about the uniqueness of the Harper Method. On page three Martha wrote:

"Just as our skyscrapers are built brick by brick, so the Harper Method reputation has been built up woman

by woman ... This rare reputation is loaned to you; and such a course is unusual."

Of course, the textbook taught specific techniques for giving facials, massages, shampoos, and haircuts:

"Wash your hands first."
"Comb before brushing."
"Start massage with the scalp, then neck and shoulders."
"Manicure the entire hand."
"A high forehead almost demands bangs."

Dr. Herriman's influence on Martha could also be found in the book. There were chapters on bone structure, muscles, the vascular system, the lymph system, skin, and nutrition. But the book did much more than impart knowledge; it brought to life Martha's personal philosophy of beauty as the result of good health. It interwove Christian Science principles with hairdressing techniques. After several pages of teaching skills, she wrote:

"At last we have our lady completed. She is healthy; therefore beautiful. If she will only maintain her general health now and give intelligent and regular care to her hands, face, and scalp, she may expect to remain beautiful and charming for years and years and years."

"Health, health, health is the basis of the Harper method."

Martha taught her franchisees to be role models, to lead by example.

"We sleep with our windows open. But we get out of bed as soon as we awaken—it breeds purpose and strength of character. We eat wisely, choosing a varied selection of green vegetables. We drink plenty of water."

"...always abide by the principles of truth, thoroughness, and good faith. Any institution conscientiously adhering to these principles must prosper."

Having an excellent product is not enough to keep a business going. Every business owner must know how to sell her product and attract new customers. Martha's textbook offered this advice for increasing sales.

"Sell as you are using a product—describe what you are doing and why."

"Your customer is not doing you a favor by buying Harper Method Preparations from you; she is benefiting herself."

Martha believed in advertising by direct mail and in newspapers. Potential customers were to be found in the city Blue Book, club memberships, and names in the society news. Operators were advised against paying someone else to do their advertising for them.

"Do not let yourself be talked into altering your course by some smooth-tongued spell-binder who draws a nice, fat commission for separating you from your money."

The textbook ended with Martha's personal story as if to say, "I overcame poverty and servitude to become a successful business owner. You can do it, too." Martha was certainly someone to emulate.

The Harper enterprise had become an empire. By 1926, there were over 500 Harper Method salons all over the United States, Canada, and Europe. There were two laboratories making 1,000 gallons of tonic a month. Celebrities, presidents, first ladies, and heads of state came to Harper salons throughout the world for pampering.

500 Shops!

Five Training Schools!

Presidential favor!

Martha Matilda Harper had arrived!

No one in America was prepared for what happened next.

127

Chapter 21

The Great Depression

When the stock market crashed in October, 1929, America sank into an economic depression. Wealthy people lost fortunes overnight. Many working-class people lost their jobs. Some stood in long food lines for a cup of soup, their daily meal. Not everyone was affected in the same way, but many women no longer had extra money to spend on their face and hair.

Martha met this challenge as she had met other challenges in the past—head-on. While the national mood became as depressed as the economy, Martha refused to give in to doom and gloom. She maintained a positive attitude and encouraged her Harperites to do the same. Through her newsletter, she reminded them that the Harper goal was achieved when everyone benefitted and profited, even during the Depression. Martha urged her shops not to cut prices but to maintain the high level of operation that her customers treasured.

In the March-April 1930 newsletter, she reminded operators and owners what lowering prices meant. "If other shops want to give ... treatments for 50 cents, is that any reason why you should work for nothing?"

Marketing was Martha's strength, and it served her well when hard times threatened. She offered ideas of small price discounts during certain hours of the day or on slow days. Other ideas included encouraging children's play areas to be established in the shops so that the children liked coming to the shops, and the moms relaxed and patronized them. "Children become our future customers that way," Martha instructed.

She kept encouraging the Harperites to keep their sights on success. In the July-August, 1930 issue of *Harper Method Progress,* Martha wrote, "Just stick to the Harper Method and good old-fashioned principles, and you'll wear diamonds of your own making. Then you can go to Europe or do anything else you want."

Another newsletter featured statements from Harperites who talked about their pride in putting their children through school or buying themselves pearl necklaces. With this "believe it and you will achieve it" philosophy, the business stayed strong, even in the weak economy. At the end, it was an inside threat, rather than an outside threat, that caused a business decline.

Chapter 22

Jubilee

In 1932, at the age of seventy-five, Martha was getting tired. The short, feisty ball of fire was losing energy, so she turned over the presidency of the business to her husband, Robert. Martha became Vice President and Founder. In her newsletter, Martha urged her "girls" to stay loyal to the company.

She wrote, "The past year I have felt it my duty, as well as my great privilege, to remain strictly and absolutely on the job all the year—so that I might hold myself in readiness for my pressed girls. Loyalty, to my mind, is one of the most essential virtues. Beware of all such temptations to cut loose and follow an independent course."

With Robert MacBain now in charge, the Harper Method began to change—as evidenced at the production meetings. "Captain," the laboratory manager said at one such meeting, "I'm reading in the news and in the trade magazines that all the salons are giving permanent waves now. Shouldn't we be offering this, too, in order to keep up with the competition?"

George, another long-term employee disagreed. "Permanent waves take away the natural beauty of the hair, and they're not healthy. You know how Miss Harper feels about that. She's always been against harsh, artificial treatments."

Robert thought a minute and said, "Perhaps we can compromise. Let's see if we can't come up with a permanent wave that is gentle on the hair."

"We can try," said George, "but, Captain, you're going to have to be the one to get Miss Harper to approve."

"If it puts the company ahead, I think she'll see that we have to do it."

The men had their way, and Harper permanent waves were being advertised as the "safe" way to curl hair.

A few years later another big compromise was made when Harper's company launched the Martha Method Hair Crayon for ladies who wanted to make their gray hair less conspicuous. This was another practice that Martha had strongly argued against, but now she was watching another ideal go down the drain.

Slowly the company's philosophy changed from "our products will release your inner beauty" to "our products will make you beautiful," a subtle but important difference. Still, the business thrived.

In 1938, when Congress passed the Federal Food, Drug, and Cosmetic Act, cosmetics became more carefully examined than drugs. When salons were forced to be inspected and to label ingredients in their products, the Harper salons didn't mind at all. Because of Martha's insistence on scientific methods and organic products, her salons were ahead of their time and easily met government regulations and earned the Good Housekeeping seal of approval. Their competitors did not.

The five Harper training schools were also a source of pride for the company. The schools were so well-respected that competitors were luring away the trainees to their own salons.

So, in 1938, after fifty successful years in the business, it was time for a celebration, and Martha was nervous. Robert found her in the second floor dormitory checking the beds for clean sheets.

"Mattie, what are you doing up here in this heat?"

Martha pulled the coverlet back over the top of the bed. "I want things to be just so for our guests. I want my girls to feel special when they come here."

"I know, Mattie, that's why you're so special yourself, but you have a maid to do this for you now." He gently nudged Martha toward the door. At age eighty-one, Martha wasn't moving as fast as she used to. She paused in the doorway for a look back at the room.

"Robbie, can you believe that I once was a servant, and now I have servants of my own? That's what I want for my girls, too. I wish all of them could stay with us."

"Mattie you have four hundred girls coming. How could they all stay with us? Why, even your friend, Mrs. Roosevelt, couldn't provide beds in the White House for that many people."

"But they are coming here for a party tomorrow, right? Maybe I should check with Beatrice again."

"Mattie, just come downstairs with me. We'll sit in the garden and have some iced tea. There we can supervise the tables being set up for the festivities here. That will put your mind at ease."

She took his arm. "All right, Robbie, whatever you say."

Robert and a core group of Harperites had been planning this Jubilee Convention for weeks. It was to be a week-long party. Hundreds of salon owners and staff were expected to fill up Rochester hotels.

The sun rose early on Monday, August 22, but not as early as Martha. "You're up early," Robert said to Martha as he leaned over the breakfast table to give her a good morning kiss.

"Up early?" she replied. "I never really went to bed."

"You're not still fussing about the party are you? I told you I've taken care of everything."

"I think that it's more excitement than worry. I'm so anxious to see my old friends."

A few hours later, Captain and Mrs. MacBain were welcomed with applause as the doorman of the Hotel Seneca opened wide the massive front door, bowed from the waist, and ushered them in. The Hotel Seneca was Rochester's largest (500 rooms) and fanciest hotel right in the center of the business district. Martha had been to the hotel before and loved its French marble walls and gold trimmed columns, but today her eyes were on her girls who filled the lobby.

After many smiles and hugs and kisses, the group moved into the ballroom where Rochester Mayor Lester Rapp and Chamber of Commerce President Warren Parks officially welcomed all of the out-of-town guests. Then Captain MacBain got up to speak. He blew a kiss to his wife who was sitting in the front row. Martha returned the kiss, and sat back as he praised her strength, her courage, her kindness, and just about everything else about her. A few times she even blushed as he listed all of her accomplishments. The speeches went on.

If the morning was about Martha, the evening was about her girls, the "pioneers," who were the sixty-two women who had over twenty-five years with the company and still operated Harper Shops. They were each called up to the stage for certificates, gifts, and applause. When Miss Kathleen Sullivan came forward, Martha openly wept. Kathleen was the oldest attendee. She had been with

Martha almost from the beginning, opening her shop in St. Paul in 1897.

"If only Bertha could be here, too," Martha whispered to Robert, who sat by her side for the whole proceedings. Bertha Farquhar, Martha's first assistant and franchisee, had died in 1932.

"She's with us in spirit, dear." Robert patted Martha's hand. He always knew the right thing to say and do.

On Tuesday, the party moved to the laboratory where a long line of Harper beauty products had been carefully laid out. At the head of the line was Martha's little brown jug of hair tonic and the unique shampoo bowl. Martha slowly walked along this "Pageant of Progress," as it was called, and looked at the list of ingredients for her products and noted from where they had come. A lump formed in her throat as she identified: coconut oil from China, olive oil from Spain, herbs from Yugoslavia, lanolin from Germany, quince seed from Madagascar. The list went on. There was a display of Harper combs and brushes—brushes made with Siberian boar bristles imported from Russia. The frightened little girl from Munn's Corners, Ontario, was now doing business with people from all over the world.

Next came the parade. From the laboratory, four hundred Harperites, dressed and coifed to look their very best, marched proudly down Main Street to the MacBain home. There a garden party awaited them. Martha and

Robert had arranged for tables and tables of fancy food and for live music to entertain their guests while they ate. The Harperites returned the favor, spoiling them with extravagant gifts.

First, the shop owners presented Martha with a throne, an armchair upholstered in gold brocade, a perfect symbol of the 50th Anniversary. Martha was called forward to sit in her proper place. Robert bowed to his queen as he helped her up to the seat and then stepped away into the background. All eyes were on Martha. If anyone noticed that the lady who refused to dye a customer's hair, mysteriously never seemed to turn gray herself, they were too kind to mention it.

The gifts continued. Martha received a large silver tea and coffee set to symbolize the friendship and cooperation among all of the shop owners and operators. Then it was flowers, including fifty golden rosebuds. Finally, the crown appeared. The youngest member of the Harperite "queendom" was chosen to place a crown of flowers on Martha's head. Martha couldn't speak. She thought back to that day in the carriage, the day her parents had sent her away to become a servant. If they could only see me now, she thought. If only they could see me now.

Martha was brought back to the present when another gift was brought forward, this time for Robert. He was given a leather-bound set of the works of Scottish poet Robert Burns. It was a thoughtful gift, and Martha joined in the applause given to her very dear husband.

Martha didn't know how there could be any more, but there was. Wednesday was a day of speechmaking. At a banquet again in the Hotel Seneca, telegrams were read from around the world. Eugene VanVoorhis, son of Martha's original attorney, was the first speaker. He began by reading a greeting from New York State Governor Herbert Lehman before reminiscing about the feisty girl who had come into his father's office, insisting on opening something strange called a hair salon in the most important office building in Rochester, New York. Martha laughed at her younger self. Where had she found the courage to do that?

The tributes went on. Mrs. Meta Fay, an early customer in Washington, D.C., brought personal greetings from First Lady Eleanor Roosevelt. Mrs. Roosevelt praised Martha's humanitarian spirit and concern for other women. Martha was on top of the world!

Mrs. Steinhausen spoke last. "Miss Harper's crowning achievement is not the accumulation of wealth, but her modesty, her desire to help humanity, her vision, and her serene assurance. Many women in history have ruled through inheritance and force, but Miss Harper reigns through intelligence, service, and sacrifice."

Martha breathed a sigh of contentment, a queen surrounded by her loyal subjects. Not a beauty queen, but a queen of beauty, who encouraged other women to project their own natural beauty, and even to set up "queendoms" of their own.

Chapter 23

Growing Old

There was another announcement at the Golden Jubilee that was made with a lot less fanfare. Robert MacBain introduced the new marketing team: Earl Freese, Warren Wheeler, and James McGarvey. Martha's energy was running out, and her company, which served women and promoted women, was now being run by men. By not choosing a strong woman to succeed her, someone who held the same values as she did, who wanted to help other women become successful business owners in their own right, Martha had contributed to her company's demise. Slowly the company that had a social conscience became a more profit-driven organization.

In 1944, when Martha started showing signs of dementia, Robert spent more and more time taking care of his Mattie and less time at the business. This role of caretaker eventually wore Robert out, and he moved them from the stately mansion that had been one of the hallmarks of their success to a smaller house that didn't need so much care. He confided his frustration in a letter to his sister, Grace.

> *Dear Grace,*
> *I must report Martha is still anything but a well lady. Moreover, the doctor tell[s] me we can never hope to see her fully recovered.....The lady allows no one to help her or even touch her, except myself....For years, I've been doing all the cooking, housework, cleaning, shopping, etc.... I'll have to put little Mattie to bed and ask God to take good care of her while I too try to get a little rest.*

Martha liked having her Robbie by her side, but that didn't mean that she went along with everything he said. One thing they disagreed about was medical care. Robert believed in traditional health care while Martha clung to her Christian Scientist beliefs and relied on Diving Healing. She continued to insist on vigorously brushing her hair every day, and when she didn't have the strength to do it herself, Robert would do it for her.

Robert and Martha tried to hide her failing health from the rest of the world, and Martha managed to come out to celebrate the sixtieth anniversary of the business in 1948. She was ninety-one years old.

When Martha became ill, Robert and his niece, Esther, who was visiting at the time, made her comfortable in a special "sickroom." Then Robert called a doctor who prescribed some medicine.

"Here, Mattie. I have something to make you feel better," said Robbie. He pulled Mattie up to a sitting position and handed her a cup of water. "Just take one of these pills and a sip of water, and you'll be well in no time."

"Thank you, Robbie." Mattie put the pill in her hand, turned her head to the side and put her hand up to her mouth. Then she reached out for the cup and sipped some water. They repeated this ritual every day, and sure enough, Martha got better. It wasn't until Martha left the sickroom and Esther was cleaning up that Martha's determination to follow her own beliefs became evident. Esther was shocked to find under the bed all of the pills that Martha had only pretended to take.

Another time, Martha broke her arm. Again, Robert insisted that she see a medical doctor who put the broken arm in a cast. Her mind might not have been as sharp as it once was, but Martha had long ago decided that she would not let anyone control her life, not even her beloved Robbie. Martha dragged herself out of bed, drew herself a hot bath, and soaked her arm in the tub until she could peel the cast off.

Robert and Martha tried to hide her failing health from the rest of the world, and Martha managed to come out to celebrate the sixtieth anniversary of the business in 1948. She was ninety-one years old.

Once again three hundred Harperites and twenty-five dignitaries gathered to pay homage to Martha Matilda Harper and the Harper Empire. The president of the Rochester Chamber of Commerce declared Martha the foremost woman in Rochester. She had been the first woman allowed to join the Chamber. Martha acknowledged the adulation with smiles, and bows, and kisses blown to all the admirers.

A highlight of the celebration was the unveiling of a portrait of Martha by Renold of Beloit, Wisconsin. The crowd roared in approval when they heard that the portrait would eventually be sent to the National Portrait Gallery in Washington, D.C.

The sixtieth anniversary was Martha's last hurrah. Her health continued to decline, although at times the spirit of the feisty, young woman who dared to follow her dream and challenge the accepted social practices of her day managed to break through.

Fausta Ahrens, a visiting niece, told this story. "One night we were having dinner. Martha dressed up for dinner as she always did. Robert noticed that Martha had smeared lipstick across her eyebrows and lovingly corrected her. 'Now, Mattie, lipstick belongs on your lips, not on your eyebrows. We will have to do something about that.' Martha raised herself up in her chair, looked Robert right in the eye, and declared, 'If Martha Matilda Harper does it, the rest of the world will follow.'"

Indeed it has.

Afterward

Martha Matilda Harper died on August 3, 1950, two years after the sixtieth anniversary and one month short of her ninety-third birthday. She left her entire estate to Robert.

Robert MacBain died on April 30, 1965. Their combined estate totaled $750,000. They are buried next to each other in Rochester's Riverside Cemetery. Her stone dominates. Martha's larger stone is marked with her trademark cornucopia etched on both sides. Robert's is in front of Martha's, barely noticeable. He chose a smaller in-ground stone paid for by the government because of his military service, reflecting how proud he was of the time he served as Captain in World War I. It was a fitting choice, not only reflecting his Scottish frugality, but also acknowledging that he knew he always was in the shadow of Martha Matilda Harper, his wife and benefactor.

Seven years later, all of the Harper Method Assets were sold to PEJ Beauty Corporation, a subsidiary of the Wilfred Academy, a competing beauty school. PEJ closed down all the Harper training programs. According to Harperites, PEJ did not want to have the high Harper standards part of their own operation nor out there as an unbeatable competitor. Later, PEJ would be put out of business for corrupt practices.

A Canadian company in St. Catherine, Ontario, held the formulae for the original Harper hair products.

They are no longer produced under the Harper name. The individual Harper shops all remained open until their owners retired or died. The last Harper Method salon to close was Martha's original shop in downtown Rochester. It remained open until just a few years prior to the writing of this book

The Harper Laboratory still stands on Main Street in Rochester. Martha Matilda Harper's name is still visibly etched into the stone façade, but another company now operates there.

Would there still be a Harper Salon today if Martha had chosen a woman, a woman whom she had trained in the Harper Method, to lead the company when her health failed? There's no way to know. Trends in beauty have changed over the years like changes in clothing and changes in women's roles in life. In fact, Martha would feel right at home in today's day spas with the emphasis on organic products, wellness, and serenity. Martha and the Harper Method may be gone, but her legacy goes on.

What Exactly is Martha Matilda Harper's Legacy?

❖ As of 2000, American franchising, the business model that Martha created, accounted for more than half of all retail sales in America.

❖ By 2009, women owned 40% of businesses in the U.S., and those businesses grew at double the rate of other businesses as a whole. These eight million, women-owned enterprises had an annual economic impact of nearly $3 trillion.

❖ Salons still use reclining chairs based on Martha's design when washing hair.

❖ Today a woman's worth is more often based on what she does, but it still matters how she looks.

❖ The market for organic hair and skin products and massages continues to grow.

❖ Martha's business practices including customer satisfaction, teamwork, positive thinking, and win-win relationships have become standard practice for successful businesses.

❖ In 1890, the ratio of men to women in the beauty/hair professions was 20:1. By 1990, this had totally reversed, and women outnumbered men by a ratio of 10:1.

What can't be perfectly measured is the impact Martha had on the lives of her shop owners and their families. She took servant girls like herself and turned their lives around with business ownership and the prospect of self-reliance and self-respect. If each of the shop owners employed only three other people, it would make 2,000 women who passed on to their daughters and their daughters' daughters the idea that women could be business owners. If we take into account the customers of Harper shops, the number grows even larger. Martha's once revolutionary ideas have now become part of mainstream American life. Franchises dot the world. What Martha stated is clearly true, "If Martha Matilda Harper does it, the world will follow."

Sir Harold Evans in his book *They Made America* cited Harper as one of sixty entrepreneurs who changed America.

Harper was inducted into the National Women's Hall of Fame in 2003 and into the American Business Hall of Fame in 2014.

Shared Success

Some day you, too, might start a business with a new idea. Be encouraged to know you, too, can succeed. Use Martha's guidance, and please share your success with us!

marthamatildaharper1888@gmail.com

Ten Commandments of Business Success

© 2011 Jane Plitt

Based on: Martha Matilda Harper's Transformation from Servant to Franchise Creator

1. **Dare to Dream & Persevere**

2. **Seize Opportunity**

3. **Capitalize On Your Assets**

4. **Build Everything on Service**

5. **Commit the Customer**

6. **Innovate—Think Outside the Box**

7. **Develop Win-Win Strategies**

8. **Lead & Brand**

9. **Reward Your Staff/Customers**

10. **Celebrate Your Success**

Glossary

Abolition – the ending of—especially slavery.

Blue Book – a listing of important members of a community.

Chamber pot – a container used for bathroom functions during the night to avoid the outhouse.

Cornucopia – a container shaped like a horn or cone overflowing with fruits and vegetables.
Symbolizes abundance.

Cupola – a small structure built on top of a roof, usually round and decorative.

Declaration of Sentiments – document signed by 100 women and men at the Women's Rights Convention in Seneca Falls, NY in 1848 stating that women deserve the same rights as men.

Elixir – a sweetened medicinal drink usually containing alcohol.

Epithet – a word or phrase describing a person or place, sometimes on a tombstone.

Flapper – a woman in the 1920s who went against tradition and wore short skirts and short hair.

Henna – a plant used to make a reddish-brown hair dye.

Inheritance – a gift of money, property, or genetic characteristics passed within a family.

Lanolin – oil from lamb's wool used in ointments and cosmetics.

Mecca – a place thought of as the center of a particular group or interest, a sacred destination.

Physiology – the branch of biology that deals with living matter, organs, tissues, and cells.

Pilgrimage – a journey to a sacred place.

Soiree – a fancy party held in the evening.

Suffragist – a person who promotes women having the right to vote.

Trollop – a woman who has a bad reputation.

Trousseau – the personal possessions of a bride – clothes, accessories, household linens.

Events in Martha's Life	Year	Other Events
	1848	Wm's Rts. Convention Seneca Falls, NY
Martha Matilda Harper born	1857	
Martha is servant for Uncle John	1864	
	1872	Susan B. Anthony arrested for voting
	1879	Christian Science Religion formed
Robert Arthur MacBain born	1881	
Martha comes to America	1882	
Martha works for the Roberts	1883	
1st Harper Method Salon opens	1888	G. Eastman founds Eastman Kodak Company
2nd Harper Salon opens In Detroit	1891	
3rd Harper Salon opens In Chicago	1893	Chicago World's Fair
Harper joins Church of Christ, Scientist	1897	Grateau patents curling Iron, Marcel Wave
Robert MacBain graduates college	1910	
Martha and Robert meet at Yellowstone	1912	
MacBain joins Co. then Joins U.S. Army	1914	World War I

MacBain rejoins Co. Martha & Robert marry; 175 Franchises	**1920**	19th Amendment gives Women right to vote
Cornerstone laid for new headquarters	**1921**	
New headquarters, lab completed	**1922**	
1st newsletter: Harper Method Progress	**1923**	
MacBains move to Culver Road mansion	**1925**	
Harper Method textbook published	**1926**	
500 Harper franchises— Worldwide	**1927**	
Luella Roberts dies; Harper products sold in Dept stores	**1930**	Great Depression begins in U.S.
Robert-- Harper Method Pres.; Martha-- Vice Pres , Founder	**1932**	
1st permanents in Harper Salons	**1933**	
Harper 50th Anniversary Jubilee	**1938**	U S Food, Drug, Cosmetic Act.
Martha dies	**1950**	
Robert MacBain dies	**1965**	
Harper bought by PEJ Beauty Corp.	**1972**	

Acknowledgments

We want to thank Leia Madden and Suzanne Valentine for their pencil illustrations on the inside of the book and Vicki Rollo for the book design.

Deep appreciation to Sarah Lecount, Leatrice Kemp (now deceased) and the Rochester Museum and Science Center for providing access to Martha Matilda Harper's papers, books, beauty equipment, and her wonderful chair—which are all housed there.

Thanks also to Kelsey Curtis, Kathy Eppeira, Kenidi Galloway, Patricia Homier, Theresa Homier, Gabrielle Lahoda, Abigail Lamphier, Tina Lamphier, Reyna Ottnod, Ally Walker, and Mary Zadorozny for reading this manuscript and providing valuable feedback.

Finally, thanks to Clarissa Thomasson and Brenda Spalding for formatting and uploading the manuscript.

About the Authors

Jane Plitt

Jane Plitt is the author of the adult biography of Martha Matilda Harper, *Martha Matilda Harper and the American Dream*, which propelled Harper back into business history, the National Women's Hall of Fame, and the American Business Hall of Fame. Sir Harold Evans in his book, *They Made America*, cited Harper as one of sixty entrepreneurs who changed America. He made a TED talk about Harper and franchising. 100,000 people have viewed it. https://www.youtube.com/watch?v=Ie8qJuXYN7w

In 2017, she wrote *Martha's Magical Hair*, a compelling young children's picture story about Harper that has been embraced by the Campaign for Grade Level Reading. As a Visiting Scholar at the University of Rochester, an award-winning businesswoman, and a recognized champion of women's rights, she has deep commitments to these causes.

Plitt is passionate about sharing Harper's wisdom and the legacy Harper offers all people in transforming their lives and the lives of others regardless of race, religion, gender, ethnic background and the like. Check out the Harper website www.marthamatildaharper.org , like Harper's Facebook page, and sign-up for the Harper newsletter. Plitt has spoken to audiences around the world and welcomes such opportunities. Contact her at marthamatildaharper1888@gmail.com

Sally Valentine

Sally Valentine is the author of a series of middle-grade novels: *The Ghost of the Charlotte Lighthouse, Theft at George Eastman House,What Stinks?, Lost at Seabreeze*, and *STORMED*. Her book of poems, *There Are No Buffalo In Buffalo,* won first prize in the Writer's Digest Self-Published Book Awards in the category of middle-grade/young adult.

As a teacher with over thirty years of classroom experience, Valentine regularly speaks in front of schoolchildren, library groups, teacher groups and book clubs. She has written study guides to go with all of her books. The guides are available on her website www.RochesterAuthor.com. She has always been fascinated by Martha's story, and hopes to inspire today's youth to dream big, work hard, and make a difference in the world. This is a timeless tale.

You may contact Valentine at mstgsl@aol.com

Made in the USA
Columbia, SC
30 May 2018